Paul —

Some light reading

for your

retirement.

A

What are people saying about this book?

"For those managers who have struggled to make it happen, get it done, and transform strategies into business growth, here's the missing medicine from an expert. Alizabeth offers a prescription—it comes down to realism and, above all, growing up!"

Jacoline Loewen
Managing Director
Loewen & Partners Inc.

"Growing Up is an interesting and readable book. The point that Alizabeth makes about business development resembling human development is clever. If you have not had quality early development, you will probably fail in your grown-up business development."

Dr. J. Fraser Mustard
The Founders Network

"Growing Up has some amazing life lessons. I'd like a copy for all of my clients."

Paul King, Gestalt Therapist

"Alizabeth's book is brilliant and amazing. The concept of toddler to maturity is an analogy that powerfully can get across to business people what they need to do to succeed. The book is helping me see the missing pieces that cause much of the mediocrity and big problems in my businesses—and then helps restore with the correct remedies to create success."

Bruce Painter,
Author of *The Giving Zone*
Host of Giving Zone Radio
Business Momentum Coach

"*Alizabeth has taken the art of leadership to a new level.* Growing Up *weaves two of life's greatest challenges, parenting and business leadership, together to form a marvellous tapestry of lessons targeted to the office but as valuable in the home. Drawing from a breadth of experience as Fortune 500 executive, consultant and parent, she provides market and life-tested advice for anyone faced with the challenge of inspiring others to great achievement. If improving your leadership game is your goal…Read On!*"

P. Bruce Hunter, CEO Coach and author of
Fog Lights: Piercing the Fog of Everyday Business

"*After 20 years of growing my business, I find* Growing Up *to be an imaginative and insightful look at how entrepreneurs can build their businesses.*"

Judith Humphrey, President and Founder,
The Humphrey Group

"*Are you a Toddler, Adolescent or Independent Adult in Business? The answer may in fact surprise you. Read this book to recognize how your company actually operates and receive guidance on how to quickly transition to the next level. Through tales of what we do intuitively as parents,* Growing Up *applies a fresh perspective and common sense approach to the needs of every growing business. Alizabeth provides a practical handbook for building a strong sustainable business that is a must read for every business manager.*"

Stefanie Hartman, CEO
www.PrivateJVClub.com

Growing Up

Practical Strategies for
Sustainable Business Growth

Alizabeth Calder

First Edition

Multi-Media Publications Inc.

Oshawa, Ontario

Growing Up:
Practical Strategies for Sustainable Business Growth
by Alizabeth Calder

Managing Editor:	Kevin Aguanno
Copy Editing:	Charles Sin
Typesetting:	Peggy LeTrent
Cover Design:	Troy O'Brien

Published by:
Multi-Media Publications Inc.
Box 58043, Rosslynn RPO
Oshawa, ON, Canada, L1J 8L6

http://www.mmpubs.com/

Hardcover	ISBN-10: 1-55489-045-4	ISBN-13: 9781554890453
eBook Formats	ISBN-10: 1-55489-046-2	ISBN-13: 9781554890460

Published in Canada. Printed simultaneously in the United States of America and the United Kingdom.

CIP data available from the publisher.

Table of Contents

Growing Up

Growing Up with People and Process

Dedication

To Geoffrey and Avery. You are my inspiration.

Introduction

> *"The biggest adventure you can ever take is to live the life of your dreams."*
>
> —Oprah Winfrey

As we grow up, from taking the first stumbling steps, to learning to communicate, and on to adulthood, the world evolves from a blank slate of endless possibilities to a more defined range of options. What options we have is a unique and individual thing—enabled by our ability and the experience and training we've had. Yet, from those first steps, some of us will become the next Warren Buffett, and others will lead unremarkable lives, or even fail. The parenting and guidance we received in our formative years can have a major impact on our chances of success.

The formation and growth of new companies follows a similar path, from the initial birth and euphoria of a brilliant idea, to the building of a business plan, obtaining the financing to go into business, and then the growth and maturing of the business into a vibrant enterprise.

Yet, as with people, few businesses achieve outstanding success. Many of them remain in the middle ground or eventually die away from hardening of the company arteries.

The objective of this book is to apply what we've learned from the experience of parenting to starting, growing and maintaining your business.

> *I left IBM to go to a significantly smaller business. Overnight, I found myself in the 'surprise a day' program. After a few weeks, I finally realized that I needed to stop saying 'we do what?' and 'we don't do what?' It never dawned on me that so many mature disciplines that I took for granted—what to do and how to do it—were not generally known or practiced.*

> *I started to look more closely at the small business experiences around me. Not just my company, but others. Some companies are successful in spite of the gaps. Some companies were not succeeding, but didn't know why. I even found companies that were struggling and understood that 'maturity' was at the core of their challenge—they actually said 'we need to grow up'—but they didn't know how to make that change.*

> *'Growing up' is daunting taken as a single challenge, but taken in steps, it's actually pretty easy. How to build the steps to make it easy to understand and straightforward to execute? This book started to form in my mind.*

> *When I began to actually put pen to paper, I had a binder full of thoughts and experiences—*

*anecdotal bits that, properly structured, can
fundamentally change the playing field for a
small business. I had drawn the child raising
analogy in my mind but needed to make it
real on paper. At a loss for how to start, I did
what any self-respecting parent would do and
asked my kids for help. They understood what
I wanted to say! Not only did they understand,
my daughter Avery actually worked with me to
think of examples of things I had done when they
were growing up that she thought related to the
business dimension.*

*This is it. If a sixteen-year-old girl can see
the parallel, you can make it work.*

In *Sun Tzu and the Art of Business*, Mark McNeilly
talks about the attributes of character-based leadership:

- *"Motivate both emotionally and materially*

- *Lead with actions, not just words*

- *Build your character, not just your image*

- *Share your employees' trials, not just their triumphs*

- *Assign clearly-defined missions; avoid confusion"* [1]

Effective parents strive to achieve exactly the same
attributes in their children. Just turn the thinking around, and
use effective parenting techniques to help your business grow.

CHAPTER ONE

What You Need To Do Next Depends on Where You Are Now

A Maturity Profile

*"If aliens visited our planet today, they might
easily assume that toddlers are pretty stupid.
Toddlers can't feed themselves well, have little in
the way of spoken language skills, and exhibit
a wanton disregard for sharp table corners.
Indeed, they don't have the sense to avoid obvious
environmental dangers such as hot stoves and
big brothers. When provoked, they just sit on the
floor and cry. Aliens would surmise that toddlers
are inferior. But we know better.*

*Many businesses, government institutions,
school systems and associations are very much like
toddlers, full of potential and promise. They are
not inherently stupid; it's just that the concept
of an organization is so new to this world that*

15

> *they may not be able to fully fend for themselves.*
> *To reach their full potential, toddlers need true*
> *parenting, not just caretaking.*" [2]

As with kids, the rate and pace of a business maturing will vary. We've all met kids who are mature in some respects, and not in others. We've all met grown ups who are immature. That's the nature of growing up. What's important for a business is the difference—to be deliberate in where 'grown up' behavior will be important, and then to focus on those grown up skills.

Most of what we do as parents is relatively intuitive—training and discipline—what things to do, and how to do them. The same applies for your business. You can leverage the most basic parenting instincts to get your business maturity to where you need it to grow.

A company's business maturity is a product of the things that they've dealt with—the specific disciplines that experience has demanded they build. If they've been through a few big projects, their team may be very mature in metrics, planning and managing change. If they've been through a few acquisitions, their processes and people strategies may be more mature because they needed to integrate.

What you need to do next depends on where you are now.

I was at IBM during the Lou Gerstner years. In his book *Who Says Elephants Can't Dance*[3], Lou says "If you ask me today what single accomplishment I am most proud of in all my years at IBM, I would tell you this – that as I retire, my successor is a longtime IBM'er, and so are the heads of all our major business units… I just had to find the teammates who were ready to try to do things a different way."

IBM, for example, personifies a mature people strategy—probably too mature for what the business needed to do. When Lou joined IBM what we really needed was to deal with the mid-life crisis:

- We needed to let go of our white knuckled grip on middle age.

- We needed to embrace some of the good things that combine the vigor of youth with independent adulthood.

- We needed to remember how to be fact based, and let go of the folklore about how things had always been done.

- We needed to be participative to get at the people and ideas that would restore us to growth.

In many respects we needed to be less mature.

How Old Do You Think I Am ?

When Bill Gates started Microsoft in the 80's, he hired Frank Gaudette as Microsoft's first ever Chief Financial Officer. Gaudette was the start-up leader for just about everything that wasn't product development or sales. Often described as a crusty old cigar-smoking New Yorker, Gaudette was a solid old-school finance and operations guy. For years he was Microsoft's oldest employee. Microsoft CEO Steve Ballmer tells the story of the first time he and Gates ever argued—Ballmer wanted to hire 17 people, but Gates' policy, no doubt Gaudette's doing, was to always have enough money in the bank to operate for a year with no revenue. Under Gaudette's tutelage, the young Gates was convinced that anything less would put him on the brink of bankruptcy.

Gates was smart enough to hire someone to take a strong 'parental' role. Gaudette looked after the starting up and sustainability of everything else, so that Gates could let himself focus on product development and innovation. Most of us don't have the luxury to hire some one to 'be the grown up'—we have to figure it out for ourselves.

While there's no single or definitive scale, we can look at some basic business dimensions to characterize maturity. Consider the table in Figure 1.1. Think about where you are now. The profile isn't specific or directed at either the 'age' or the 'size' of the organization, but a point of reference for representative behaviors and attributes.

You pick the level of maturity that is sustainable and supports where you want your business to be.

A 'toddler' is growing quickly, full of promise, and relatively unaware of the consequences of some of the things he might do. He needs encouragement and support along the way – and he needs to be allowed to make some mistakes and given the guidance to learn from them.

A 'teenager' may look and even talk like an adult. She can be very responsible and very clever, but she can also be distracted and unfocused. She probably has lots of 'attitude' because she believes that she is smarter than the rest of the world – and she'll grow out of it. She has to test boundaries to learn, but her potential is limitless.

An 'adult' has earned the right to do it their way. He gets to decide whether to own a home and have a family or travel the world and focus on himself. He has control over his resources. He owns the outcomes of his decisions. We may not agree with his decisions, but it's his life.

Once we get to 'middle age,' we either gracefully accept our wrinkles and sore knees—sit back and relax a bit—or we

Business Dimensions	Toddler	Teenager	Independent Adult	Arguably Middle Aged
Contracts & Metrics	May be unknown; Recognize may be of value	Learning from experience	Fact based with effective reporting	Proactive focus on improvement and learning
Process	Not formal concept; Gradual investment—not readily seen as affordable	Largely consistent and predictable; some exception handling	Processes followed; Preventive actions taken	Proactive focus on next opportunity
Making Change	No organized activities; Take obvious and motivational approach	Understand what to do – don't always do follow through	All functions are open and receptive to suggestion and improvement	Proactive thought leadership
Planning and Managing for Growth	Ad Hoc; Emphasis on closing the next sale	Action plans established; may include communication; more cross-business focus	Participative programs that align the business; led at an executive level	Continuous activity treated as an opportunity to develop the next group of leaders
People Strategies	Individual; some focus on teams as natural groupings	Focus on being more supportive and helpful	Individuals recognize roles and take responsibility	Essential part of the company systems
Communication	Intuitive; Relationship based	Personal currency becomes important	Discretion and integrity respected throughout the organization	Mature and well governed
Decision Making	Short term focus; Can be Directive	Increased orderly and open problem resolution	Problems anticipated or recognized early	Adaptive approach ensuring thought leadership
Leadership	Relationship Influenced Dictatorship	Authenticity critical	Competence critical	Recognized strength

Figure 1.1 – A Maturity Profile

indulge in a little mid life crisis. A nip here, a trainer there, and all of a sudden we're 40 again.

There is no inherently "bad" place to be as a growing company. You just need to know where you are, and understand the tradeoffs you may be making. For example, if your people strategies, communication and leadership are all in the toddler to teenage part of the chart, you may have a harder time attracting or retaining top industry talent. If your processes and metrics aren't well aligned with what you need to get done, you may not be in a position to ramp up when that breakthrough opportunity presents itself.

Find the boxes that best describe how you work most often. Then think about whether your business can get the success you're after if that is the maturity level being managed to. Be brutally honest – ask your Executive team what they think. Pick the spots where change can get you the most bang for the buck, and make a commitment to growing up.

> *"If you always do what you always did, you're always going to get what you always got."*
>
> —Val Adamo

Toddlers aren't "bad." They just haven't yet learned that walking headlong off the top step without holding the railing is not the best strategy.

Teenagers aren't "bad." It just seemed like a perfectly good idea to hop on the bus to a party without thinking about how late the bus is running and how they're going to get home. In fact, as a show of independence it's good – but the choices for getting home might be a little sketchy.

What's important, regardless of age, is that we decide to take responsibility and we look for better ways to do it next time. From a business perspective, that's what you're looking for. It's all about making 'grown up' decisions along the way. That's how you control the choices you have, and how you position your business to always make the next better decision going forward.

The early chapters of this book look at general business strategies and approaches that can be helpful regardless of age.

The business equivalent of brush your teeth and eat well – just generally good things to do.

The later chapters address more age specific tactics. How to throw away the baby gates and trust the kids to roam the house safely (metrics and process). How to keep control over the curfew (decision making and managing change). How and when to support and guide your seventeen year old going off to school alone (communication and leadership). What to do when you are in mid life crisis and want to go back to being thirty (people strategies).

Keep it all in perspective. Like raising kids, there is no single answer. 'Growing up' takes time and patience.

CHAPTER TWO

What Gets Measured Gets Done

Contracts and Metrics

My son Geoff has one chore – taking out the garbage. Garbage day is Monday, so the garbage goes out on Sunday night. The bins need to be brought back in on Monday night.

The taking out part generally happens with little or no reminder. The buckets coming back in, however, is downright painful. I tried everything from leaving nice notes to taking him away from a TV show to do it.

I was tired of feeling like a nag, so I finally told him that I wouldn't be reminding him any more. I set the deadline at Tuesday at bedtime or he would lose that week's allowance. The first week, the buckets remained at the street until Sunday.

23

Silly me.

Once it got past Tuesday at bedtime, there was no added incentive to bother bringing in the buckets at all.

The first thing I did was acknowledged to Geoff that he was smarter than me this time. Then I changed the 'deal' – going forward, he'd lose part of his allowance for each day that passed.

There's been no discussion on the problem since.

Sometimes things just need to be done. Even if you only have a couple of employees, what needs to be done, and when, needs be made clear. The more specific the requirements, the less management time and personal attention it will take. Your employees can be more effective and independent if you are clear about what 'the deal' is, and how it gets measured.

In *How to Behave So Your Children Will Too*, Sal Severe outlines the "Top Ten Reasons to Use Contracts and Metrics"[4]

1. Solidify your plan, and provide behavioral agreement.

2. Enable focus on specific and positive priorities, behaviors and attitudes.

3. Provide a record so you can evaluate progress.

4. Act as a tangible reminder for consistency.

5. Promote positive climate and encourage everyone to work together.

6. Redirect inappropriate behavior and help improve.

7. Encourage accountability.

8. Create feelings of success and internal motivation.

9. Give the child (employee) immediate positive feedback on accomplishments.

10. Give the parent (manager) immediate positive feedback on accomplishments.

The principles are the same in business. The best metrics and contracts evolve. They support both the complexity and enforcement that you need. Starting early, with some level of structure, they provide an important foundation and stability for growth. Even if you only define and measure a few key things that have to happen, your employees will be clear on what has to get done and what results you need.

> *"You can't win if you don't keep score."*
>
> —Sal Severe

You won't get to go back later and renegotiate existing contracts simply because your business has grown and you've learned a few things. You can, however, position yourself to make progress by starting now to focus on two things:

1. Metrics and contracts for managing your people;

2. Metrics and contracts for managing your other relationships (clients, suppliers).

It will be easier to define what you expect and need with your employees than with your clients, but there are things you can do to anticipate issues and at least hold a well understood negotiating position even with clients.

Metrics and Contracts for Managing Your People

Mark and Sally started in sales on the same day at Luxury Cars Ltd, a used car dealership specializing in executive leased and gently pre-owned cars. Sally was an experienced car salesperson although not in luxury cars, and Mark was straight out of school but a real sports car buff.

Bob, the owner of Luxury Cars, outlined the three things he wanted to review with them weekly:

- *Sales*

- *Number of test drives taken*

- *Number of repeat visits/come backs*

Sally objected to being micro managed, so Bob agreed to back off the measurements for one month, and then they would revisit.

Mark and Bob talked about the measurements a bit more, and agreed on a set time every week to talk about how it was going.

In the first week, Sally had one sale and Mark had no sales but 11 test drives. In the second week, Sally had one sale and Mark had one sale, 4 repeat visits and 10 new test drives. In the third week, Sally had one sale, and Mark had 9 repeat visits, 12 new test drives and 2 sales. In the fourth week, Sally had one sale and Mark had 7 repeat visits, 9 new test drives and 3 sales.

Sally 4; Mark 6.

Bob had set out his three measurements for a reason. He believed that luxury buyers are more likely to come back if you can get them to drive the car. If they come back for a second look, they're even more likely again to actually make the purchase. At that point, the car has become personal. Bob's focus on the 'metrics' was not about micro management, but about what activities he thought would drive success. Mark paid attention and applied the theory, and it was working.

Smaller companies often avoid specific directed measurements, for fear of being too rigid or seeming bureaucratic. If your measurements or metrics support what needs to get done, you'll find a balance. For example:

- A jeweler knows that if a couple is looking at diamond rings, and 'the bride' doesn't try one on relatively quickly, they'll go elsewhere. They may cluck a lot, but they'll walk out the door. The jeweler that gets the first ring actually on her finger will probably make the sale – even if it is not the first ring she tried. An appropriate target for a person working in a jewelry store would be ALWAYS get a ring on the finger of the potential 'bride.'

- For most industries, there are benchmarks on how many calls it takes to get to a certain number of orders. There are usually also benchmarks on the number of orders it takes to drive a dollar value in sales. For a commission-compensated sales person, these industry benchmarks are important. It defines how many calls they have to make to make enough commission.

By measuring the things that you know result in success, you can help the more junior people know what to focus on. Keep it simple and target what you know will deliver results.

Third Party Metrics and Contracts

Lisa is a wholesale rep for Creative Automotive, a specialty aftermarket supplier for custom car accessories. Her target is for 40 calls a month, and she is making 50. Her company's average close rate suggests that 1 in 4 calls will get a direct order, and she is closing 1 out of 3. At the average $100,000 per order, her sales and commissions are well above target.

Unfortunately, Lisa's client receivables are averaging 90 to 120 days. She regularly and unwittingly calls on clients who are significantly past due, and sends them more product, when they haven't paid for recent deliveries. Nothing in Lisa's contract identifies any responsibility on her part for receivables or collections.

Lisa didn't know which clients were in arrears, and nothing had told her to have these discussions while she was out on sales calls. Creative needed to change both the metrics Lisa sees and the contract, to make sure that Lisa had the right information and the right overall targets.

For over a year, Lisa had been working with Rod Johnson at Hot Rod Incorporated. His business was growing fast, and he was more than half of her monthly sales. Unfortunately, Rod's A/R with Creative was 120 days plus. The Creative

Automotive contract specified net 30 days, but had no penalties. With the growth plans for Hot Rod Inc, Lisa was hesitant to cut him off.

Once she knew that it was her problem to solve, Lisa took the problem to Rod in a positive and proactive way. She learned that Rod was bringing his stock into his primary store, and then re-sending it on to his smaller locations, to keep control and to reduce the need for storage space in the local outlets. His payment delays were linked to the fact that his actual product turnover was 120—130 days.

By understanding Rod's problem, Lisa could offer more of a "just in time" shipment capability, direct to the local outlets, saving Rod effort and cost and making his inventory turnover something that they both could influence.

Lisa committed to < 5 days delivery time direct to the local outlet. In exchange, Rod signed a new agreement with a net 30 days commitment and a penalty clause.

It isn't uncommon for contracts that were signed in the early days of a business to have some things missing or not well thought through. This can be the case for both clients and suppliers. Specific and measurable targets, such as payables, invoicing timeliness and accuracy of documentation are important to provide a baseline to work from.

When you're looking at your contract, there are two potential areas of risk:

- **The risks you carry based on decisions your client or provider might make in the future –** what 'rules' can they change or what can they do that could leave your business exposed?

- **The risks that you carry based on volume –** what if you are hellishly successful?

1. What Rules Can They Change?

AccuTemp, a provider of contract based accounting and finance personnel, achieved a major milestone when they signed Gigantico Bank as a major client. As does any bank, Gigantico had very defined processes for cost reporting, and they required that all contractor time be billed within 3 months of the time / service delivery. AccuTemp had no such terms in the contracts that were already in place with their more than 1,000 contract professionals.

In their second year of working with Gigantico, an AccuTemp contractor submitted approved timesheets and an invoice to cover the full period of a 12 month contract. AccuTemp had done nothing to reset these expectations with their contractors, and they were unable to invoice Gigantico beyond the most current 3 months, although they had to to pay the contractor for the full 12 month period.

Make sure that your client's terms flow through to your supplier's terms. Think about what future client terms may demand, and make your most stringent client terms your own 'high water mark' for any subordinate contracts.

- Pay close attention to jurisdictions in case you have to litigate.

- Where metrics are linked to financial penalties, be sure to understand how those metrics are defined and delivered.

- Understand the process for changing or adding new requirements.

By monitoring your 'high water mark,' you'll quickly recognize a new client or supplier contract that is looking for more than you want to commit. Your base contract can be the trigger for you to look at gaps you might have across the board.

2. What if you are hellishly successful ?

AccuTemp decided to broaden it's business to include 'IT staffing' – contract based project managers, programmers and core technical skills. In order to quickly build a bench, they bought a small company called TechTalent. All of the TechTalent consultants were brought over under TechTalent's original contract terms, which were inconsistent and not well understood. None of the existing contracts were re-done under AccuTemp terms.

AccuTemp's strong reputation, and the strong talent pool acquired from TechTalent, quickly made AccuTemp the IT talent provider of choice for many of their existing clients.

When AccuTemp added the TechTalent consultants, they also used TechTalent's business model for terms and management approach.

> *Unfortunately, they didn't realize that Tech-Talent's terms didn't align with their planning assumptions. As the business grew, the margin gap widened quickly, leaving AccuTemp management with a significant erosion in the business results.*

Be aware of every contract gap, even minor ones. You can chose to ignore it, but when exposed to exponential business growth a minor gap can fundamentally change your business outcome. Assess all of your contracts and commitments, and the planning models behind them. Find ways to renegotiate Terms and Conditions that won't scale to your needs.

In her book *A Nation of Wimps; The High Cost of Invasive Parenting*, Hara Estroff Marano talks about "what parents can do for kids."[5] She suggests parents let kids "find for themselves the rewards of doing well." She emphasizes the difference between excellence, a self motivated focus on doing things well, and perfectionism, a stress inducing anxiety about always getting 100%. Let's learn from that – metrics don't have to be perfect—they have to be relevant.

None of us wants a company full of nervous and indecisive yes-men, but a grown up company also can't afford a group of cowboys. Use clearly defined metrics to keep the balance between initiative and prudence. Help your employees enjoy what they're doing and feel confident by being clear on what's needed and the boundaries. Then you can get out of their way.

CHAPTER THREE

Pick Your Battles

Having Effective Process

My son Geoff has never really needed prompting on deadlines for school, and he gets the full credit for his good marks. When he brought home his first high school report card, he had a better than 90% average.

As we got close to his first set of mid term exams, the teachers were spending most of the class time on review and extra help. Geoff asked if he could 'skip' these review classes, because they were really boring given that he knew the work. He thought he could make better use of the time working on his golf swing.

I wanted to give him credit for the fact that he didn't need the reviews. I also wanted to reward him for asking permission instead of just skipping. I didn't want him to think that it was going to be a free-for-all on what classes he needed to attend.

*My answer was "I think that you've earned
the right to make the decision, but I do need you
to continue to take responsibility for your grades."*

We figured out a two step process:

1. *He ALWAYS call me and tell me when
he is going to miss class, so I don't have
any surprises when the school office calls.*

2. *He checks after, with classmates or the
teacher, to make sure that he hadn't
missed anything.*

*It worked. Geoff didn't feel that I was
imposing rules or second guessing his ability to
decide, and he kept a strong personal sense of
responsibility for his work.*

Often what we call a 'rule' with children is really just a
very specific process. There are two key things to look for:

1. Make sure that it makes sense – Have an effective
process

2. Make sure that it is followed or enforced – Make
the process work

Having An Effective Process

I've seen lots of companies invest in manuals that never get
looked at. They weren't meaningful and relevant when they
were being developed, so no surprise that they're also not
meaningful or relevant when they're done. Instead, everyone
has a general idea of how they think things should be done.
If in doubt, people just ask the person at the next desk. Over
time, whatever defined 'process' there is gets further and further
away from what was intended.

I've also seen companies with a relatively simple but documented flow diagram—even just some basic defined steps—that make it clear what needs to happen, in what order, and where decisions, approvals and paperwork are required. Those lists and flow charts are often found posted on the walls of work areas and they are either well known or frequently referred to. In those companies, the critical things happen the way that they are intended to, and they happen more or less the same way every time.

Process can be basic, if you follow three simple rules:

1. **Be clear about what needs to be done.** Processes need to be very clear and only address what is truly necessary. They need to define the tasks required, the order they need to be done in (where order is important), and what documentation is required.

2. **Monitor how it's working against what you needed as an outcome.** Understand the outcome you are truly after, and how to measure or monitor that. How is the process tied in to the metrics ? By having the process and metrics aligned, when there is an exception you'll know. Then you can understand why the exception happened, and fix the process.

3. **Make sure that the process has an owner or champion.** Unless a process has someone of authority with a specific outcome in mind, you won't know if it's working. The best way to make sure that everyone is using the process effectively is to make sure that they understand why they follow the process in the first place. The owner or champion makes sure that there's clear line of sight to the business requirement.

The 'earning the right to skip class' process had two clear steps and one clear outcome. Only once in two years did I get a call from the office that was a surprise. At that point, my experience said that Geoff was managing the process responsibly, so when the office called and I hadn't heard from him, I knew that there'd be a good explanation. It turned out that his cell phone was in his locker, and the teacher had seen him in the hall, so he needed to go to the office before going to his locker to call me.

Four years later, Geoff still calls me in advance of 'skipping,' the school office is always satisfied with my response, he still has a 90% average, and his golf handicap has significantly improved. I never have to nag on any subject related to his work being complete or his grades being important.

When my daughter Avery started high school, she brought home a 90% average on her first and all subsequent report cards – up from an 80% level in Grade 8. She wasn't sure where the line was, but she wanted to also 'earn the right.'

Let your process make sense. If one person handles all aspects of the mail, accounts payable and bookkeeping you need a different process than if you have an active receiving dock sending paperwork to an accounts payable person who receives and commits payment on the invoice. Like metrics, processes will evolve because what needs to get done will evolve.

> *"A smart (process) can work with a little stupidity, but a stupid (process) can't work with even a lot of smarts."*
>
> —Steven S. Little

Making the Process Work

Now that you have effective processes in place, you need to make sure that they are effective against the 'outcome.' How do you enforce them?

> *When Geoff was a little boy, we had a 'process' around staying up after bed time. If he wanted to, for example, stay up an extra half hour for a tv show, the process was:*
>
> 1. *Ask permission*
>
> 2. *IF getting up that morning was not a battle, so I could assume that he was well rested, the answer would be yes*
>
> 3. *IF getting up had been a battle that morning, the answer would be no*
>
> 4. *The next morning, having been allowed to stay up the extra half hour, I would also assess whether there was a challenge getting up, so that I could again assess whether he had enough sleep*
>
> 5. *IF there was a challenge the next morning, Geoff then owed back the half hour, and bedtime would be that much earlier that night*

Outcomes desired were threefold… 1. Make sure that Geoff got enough sleep, 2. Make it easy for mommy to get everyone ready in the morning, and 3. Have the kids own the consequences if they're tired in the morning after they stayed up late.

We lasted a good few years on this process.

Then, one day, Geoffrey and his sister Avery had stayed up late to watch a tv show, and then they were both very crabby the next morning. That night, when we started toward bed a half an hour early as a result, and Geoff decided to sit on the stairs and refuse to go (and of course his baby sister went along with him on that decision).

Once I kept myself from laughing out loud at the sheer determination and commitment on his little face, I bought some time by saying "fine, you have one minute to think about it. If you haven't moved by then, you lose a half hour tomorrow night as well." (As the undisputed owner of the process, I get to add to it!)

There was no discussion or negotiation. I just went back to the kitchen and did my chores. Every minute I came back to the staircase to note that another minute had passed, and they each owed me another half hour the next night. Avery finally got up and went to bed after the third one minute warning. It took Geoff one more minute, and he had worked up to a full two hours early to bed the next night. When he went, he did so with no further discussion.

In his book *The Secrets of Discipline; 12 Keys for Raising Responsible Children*, Ronald G. Morrish emphasizes that "when you undertake the task of establishing (processes), you must make a commitment to ensuring that they are always obeyed. This requires time and energy, but there is no other way."[6]

> *"Rules worth having are worth enforcing; Behavior you ignore is behavior you permit."*
>
> —Ronald G. Morrish

Morrish emphasizes 'discipline' as the foundation for how we help children grow up to "be responsible, co-operative and productive," in what he calls a 'think for yourself world.' We can apply the same principles to get to "responsible, co-operative and productive" employees.

Morrish links child development and discipline to what's expected in the grown up world. "Every one of us must be willing to comply with certain rules and limits, whether it be for driving cars or respecting another person's property. This is the structure which allows people to live and work together in families and in communities. It allows everyone to feel safe and secure. Either people buy into this structure or they buy into chaos."[7]

If you've truly defined the process to be as simple as it can, and if it's linked to measurable results or triggers that are necessary business outcomes, then what you're asking is consistent for all, reasonable and appropriate. Give your team permission to manage it that way.

> *I was at IBM when they were getting into the 'services' business. I had five years of experience with another major consulting firm so I understood the*

need for accurate timesheets, submitted on time, so that customers could be billed and project budgets managed.

I was amazed by the push back on the part of the long term IBMers. They didn't want to fill in timesheets. Many would go weeks and months before submitting their time, and then it would take reminders and escalations.

These senior and long term IBM employees clearly linked the need to 'report time' with more junior, hourly employees, so they resented it. Unfortunately, it was tough to bill the client for services provided if you didn't know the time spent, so we really needed the process to be followed.

The first attempt at a process involved increasingly senior escalations to increasingly senior executives. If you were really late, you would have the opportunity to meet with the Vice President and explain your errant ways. Unfortunately, all that process did was re-inforce the negative feelings that caused the problem in the first place.

Finally, as painful as it was to implement, we found a way to enforce the process that put the consequences back in the hands of the employee. We implemented a '3 strikes' program. Any employee who had 3 or more timesheets that missed the cutoff would not be eligible for an 'exceptional' performance rating for that year because they clearly did not demonstrate the necessary understanding of what it would take for IBM and their business unit to be successful.

You'd need to have been an IBMer to truly appreciate how distasteful that prospect would be. While many employees complained, it did solve the problem.

None of us want to get into a 'consequences' discussion, especially in a business context. If and where you do need to impose enforcement, align the consequences with the problem.

If a process is worth putting in place – and if the outcomes are important enough to make the investment and commitment to manage the process – you need to commit to enforcement or consequences.

In his book *The Secrets of Discipline*, Morrish emphasizes that "you must be absolutely determined that your children will do what you tell them to do. You must be willing to persist until they follow through."[8]

A business environment probably permits us to be a little less absolute, but have no doubt that wavering on processes, and the enforcement programs to go with them, will have no good end result. Be open to ideas for improvement? Absolutely. Tolerate exceptions and non-compliance. Not if you plan to grow.

CHAPTER FOUR

Make It Easy For Them To Say Yes

Team Based Process Design

When my children started to ride bikes, they had to stay on the sidewalk and between the neighbor's driveways. I sat on the front lawn and watched them.

The next summer they got to go to the fire hydrant in one direction and to the bend in the street in the other direction. I could garden in the front yard and listen carefully.

Within a few years, they got to go over to the school or to friends alone. They were out of my sight and hearing. I had to trust that they knew how to manage crossing the street and being safe all on their own. Then I was free to garden in the back yard, make cookies, or sit on the porch and read a book.

43

We let children earn the right to go further by setting boundaries and watching how they behave. We watch to make sure that they are safe, but also to make sure that they show a clear understanding of what the rules are for things like cars turning into driveways and not talking to strangers. We look for evidence that they know why the rules exist, and that they understand their importance. Once they get the basic rules, we can add more complicated rules and have confidence that they can make the necessary judgments.

If your company is a 'toddler,' you may have some basic work to do to get started or catch up. No teenager wants to have boundaries that are defined in terms of neighbor's driveways. Even more mature processes need to be maintained to stay relevant – boundaries the teenager will accept on their bike are illogical once a car is available. What's important is that they start out understanding there are going to be boundaries, and that they can earn the right for those to be adjusted.

Boundary adjustment is part of managing process. The more detail there is in the process, the more management bandwidth it'll take for care and feeding. The KISS principle will serve you well, in both your early process efforts and to help you adjust processes as you grow. Use well aligned metrics that keep track of successful outcomes as your guide to the process' effectiveness.

Team Based Process Design

Introducing process to an undisciplined organization can be a major challenge. Some people may have a very hard time making the change to a process-based world. Once you start in, it's important not to be deterred. Taking a team based approach can help you get through it.

Include the people who will be most affected by the process. It may take a little longer, but by permitting active input on both the process and the enforcement, you make sure that those affected understand the issues. When you're finished, the whole team is better positioned to support the changes that you're trying to make.

A team effort recognizes and respects everyone's experience and knowledge, which makes it all the more difficult. Everyone will have different biases and approaches that they think are 'best.' Have a few ground rules for the team effort:

1. **Plan the work and work the plan.** Set a schedule for the work to be done, with specific milestones for completion. Keep the team on schedule. It is easy to try to 'boil the ocean' in process development.

2. **Have an owner.** Have the process owner or champion actively involved, even if just for milestone reviews of the work, to emphasize the importance and the business commitment.

3. **Expect the required people to either engage or live with what's decided.** Decide who should have input at the start of the project. Give them the opportunity to participate, or to assign their authority to someone already involved. Do not allow delegation where it alters the balance of authority in the room or diminishes the

perception of importance for the project. Instead encourage them to 'assign' their authority for input to someone else who is already represented on the team. Then the onus is on them to either participate or to stay closely aligned with their assignee.

4. **Keep discussions focused.** Pay attention to consistency in level and role. More junior people may have detailed discussions than the senior managers should (or want to) participate in. You may end up with disjointed or frustrating discussions. All levels may not need to participate as a single team. Use working groups where it makes sense to discuss more detail.

5. **There are no mistakes—encourage learning and continuous improvement.** Set a schedule to monitoring the process after you put it in place, and re-group the team to make sure that it's delivering the expected outcomes. Be open to continuous improvement and build any improvements that you need as a team.

6. **Measure the effectiveness.** Address both the process itself, and the compliance requirements. Test the resulting process to make sure that the result is linked to the outcome. Make sure that the process defines a few things you can measure, to make sure that the process is working.

7. **Keep it simple.** Some people will be looking for perfection and trying to address every eventuality and exception. Define the minimal rules that you do need; you're providing a framework – the activities need to follow a level of discipline. Consider starting with the 80/20 rule. Define the

20% of the steps that get you through 80% of the task properly, and then move forward to refine it and fill in the details.

The hardest line to draw in process work is on the amount of detail you need. If the team agrees that more detail is required, accept the recommendation—use a working team or sub-committee to build detailed parameters. The people who do the job can best understand the detailed impacts. You don't want to drag the senior team into the detail, but you also want to keep the process manageable.

Make it easy for your employees to accept a more process based world. 'What needs to be done' is a personal point of control and authority – the source of power for some people and pride for others. Your staff may think their personal knowledge is their job security. Moving toward a process-based approach may be a difficult change for your long term employees. If you think that is likely to be the case, start small and plan the work in a way that helps them come along.

In his book *The Secrets of Discipline*, Morrish talks about the example of teaching children to clean up their rooms. Many parents simply demand that the room get cleaned up. Often, hours later, nothing has been done or the other parent has taken over the nagging, with much gnashing of teeth and frustration all around. Instead, Morrish says, give direct instruction and start small. Guide the steps – "put these books on the bookshelf… put the doll with the other dolls. Bit by bit the work picks up speed."[9]

With kids, modeling the behavior and guiding the outcome is the most effective way to turn defiance into responsible and cooperative behavior. By being directive on what how and how the process will be developed, you can step back and let them do the work and own the result.

CHAPTER FIVE

What Do You Want To Be Different?

Making Change

In high school, my daughter Avery was given the opportunity to participate in a limited and invitation only program call LEAD (Leadership Enrichment and Development). The LEAD program is aimed at identifying kids with strong leadership capabilities and making those talents a true differentiator.

Her first reaction was to decline. She didn't think that the program made sense and she was concerned that her friends would think she was weird or geeky. She was also convinced that she was not a 'leader' and protested even being included.

It sounded like a great opportunity to me. She'd get the kind of leadership training that I had to work at IBM for.

Teenagers are, by nature, unsure of their talents and how they fit in the grown up world. They specifically search for boundaries and push the limits to find a frame of reference. The school was providing a supportive way to find some different context. By giving the kids specific tasks to be responsible for, and letting them figure out how to handle it, the kids would realize that they can do it themselves. By having the kids talk and write about what they'd learned, they'd relate their skills to the basic leadership concepts and understand that they are leaders after all. By practicing writing scholarship applications, they'd have to write down what makes them special.

To be included in the program, the students had to write down what they wanted to get from the course. By making them write it down, the teacher got commitment to the fact that something would be different and the kids would be part of making that change.

As I write this book, Avery is halfway through the LEAD program – one year out of two. This spring, at the meeting for the next group of grade 9 students, Avery was one of the students on stage to talk about her experience. She started with "I have to tell you that I really did not want to do this program." When a few students chuckled as if they could relate, she went on to say (as only a teenager can), "No, I mean I REALLY did not want to do this."

"But," she said, "I'm so glad I did. I'm having fun, I've learned a lot and I've made great new friends. My old friends are actually coming out to participate in some new things

because I'm involved. I'm really looking forward
to next year." What a difference a year makes.

Making change can be as simple as deciding that
there's something you want to be different, and making it
so, rather than just meandering through to wherever the day
takes you. In a business context, it can mean simply making a
decision, and making sure that everyone understands what you
had in mind. It can also be as complicated as putting together a
team of people, defining what the objective is – 'what you want
to be different' – studying what that's going to take, and then
building and acting on the plans to get there. The common
denominator is the decision that there is something you want
to be different.

In the case of the LEAD program at Avery's school, the
teachers wanted to put some extra time and effort into building
the leadership talents of the selected kids as part of the school
curriculum. They knew the approach wouldn't work for all 300
Grade 10 kids. They also knew that the kids involved had to be
committed. The LEAD program asked the 30 kids each year to
make a decision – and a risky investment. What if doing LEAD
really did cause their friends to think they were geekish? The
kids who joined were making a decision to take a risk and work
to a different level.

> *"When written in Chinese, the word*
> *crisis is composed of two characters. One*
> *represents danger, and the other represents*
> *opportunity."*
>
> —John F. Kennedy

In business, as with kids, if there is something you
want to be different you need to get the commitment you need

from the people who can make the change happen. Getting and keeping that commitment demands that you do three things:

1. Be Fact Based

2. Don't Shoot the Messenger

3. Set the Bar High

Be Fact Based

When AccuTemp signed the deal with Gigantico Bank, they were positioned to double in size almost overnight. One National deal would attract other large opportunities. Within a few months of signing the Gigantico contract, the local offices had significantly more business with customer driven tools sending out a large number of orders across the country.

They were also struggling with the more stringent customer contract terms. Consistency on contract compliance and meeting defined service level targets like response time was a new discipline for AccuTemp.

Glen was the Sales Manager responsible for Gigantico. While the local offices were responding well on the orders that they got, Glen spent much of his time asking them to provide the reporting he needed and to answer Gigantico's account management and compliance questions. As a result, he looked to the client as if he was not in control of his business.

The local offices had never really needed to cooperate on a single account before, so they had no context for Glen's requests. The general feeling in the field was that Glen was poking into their responsibilities.

The CEO knew that they needed to have compliance and reporting centrally, or they were at risk of penalties and they might not get the references that they needed to meet the sales targets. Then it would be everybody's problem. He knew that the growth plans would demand more consistent and centrally managed processes, whether they started now or later. He decided to use the opportunity they all saw in the Gigantico account to get buy-in to what the business needed to be different.

The CEO took advantage of the fact that the local offices knew the potential business they'd get if the National strategy worked. He understood that they had no experience with service level commitments and customer audits. He also knew that they had not considered the bottom line impact of fines that were potentially mounting if they didn't do what they had committed to with the Gigantico business.

The CEO at AccuTemp was close enough to his managers in the field to understand their resistance to central reporting and process. Many of them had gone so far as to express concern about Glen's seemingly intrusive approach. Giving them the benefit of the doubt, he could assume that no one local manager was trying to be mean or a create a problem—they just didn't have the experience to put it in context.

The alternate view would be that the local offices had been somewhat childish.

Either way, the local offices put the CEO in a parental role and he had to call out the problem. He took a grown up approach to correcting the relatively immature behavior.

In his book *The Secrets of Discipline*, Ronald Morrish stresses that "children learn early to shift responsibility from themselves... deny involvement. They challenge the adults to find proof."[10] The executive who accepts incomplete facts and tolerates one-sided views as a basis for making decisions and directing change is only supporting this child-like behavior.

The AccuTemp CEO needed to do the business equivalent of forcing all the kids into the room together to find out who broke the lamp. Parents have all been there—someone needs to do chores to pay for the new lamp. Either one kid would confess, one kid would squeal, or they'd all take the consequences together. The CEO needed to challenge the team, and then reign in the child-like behavior, by helping them understand all of the facts in a bigger AccuTemp context.

> *"Even if you're on the right track, you'll get run over if you just sit there."*
>
> —Will Rogers

In his book *Recreating the Workplace; The Pathway to High Performance Work Systems*, Steven R. Rayner talks about how to be successful making change. He says "be intolerant of mis-information. Be specific and fact-based. If you're making decisions about changes to be made, and investing energy and business resources toward a specific thing that you want to be different, it is critically important that you are making those decisions and directing those energies to a very specific objective."[11]

I've seen many senior executives commit to changes based on isolated feedback from one manager. Unchecked data, taken as fact, can result in a huge amount of time and effort just to get the situation back to neutral. You have to be fact based and neutral to understand what's really going on. Then you can make an informed decision about what needs to be different.

Don't Shoot the Messenger

The bearers of information need to understand the business issues being addressed, and be comfortable with the fact that they may be missing things or they may be wrong based on what they knew at the time. If there isn't that comfort level, bad news may be purified to avoid taking risk. Treat the team as a whole, and expect the whole team to be part of the solution and own the results. Learn from the team, and make challenges penalty-free, so you get adjustments as you go if you need to.

Efforts to make change, especially significant change, won't always be right the first time. If it was that easy, you'd have probably made the change long ago

Set the Bar High

Credibility, relationships and access all affect how you stay informed. In the AccuTemp example, many of the local office leaders had offered relatively negative input how Glen was handling the Gigantico account. Fortunately, the CEO was informed enough that he could take the one-sided views in context and use the inferred knowledge to develop an effective plan for change. Had he listened to the local office leaders in isolation, Glen would have had a significant challenge getting to the National model that he needed to be successful, and the whole business would have suffered as a result.

As a senior executive, you set the bar in terms of expecting openness and integrity. Don't accept part of the story—expect facts to be provided in a complete context. If you accept and act on information that isn't fact based, it affects your credibility. Expect your information sources to earn the right to be heard by paying attention to the sources you can rely on. Let your team earn the right to be heard.

Deciding on the changes you want to see in your business is critical for profitable growth. Make deliberate decisions about what changes you need to make, and stay focused on the facts that support your decision process.

Going back to Marano's book *A Nation of Wimps*, she emphasizes that it is important to let kids mess up.[12] She suggests that children need to experience a bit of discomfort in order to grow.

The same holds true in your business. Use change projects as an opportunity for people to learn and to encourage strong and responsible growth. Share your own mistakes to open the avenue for discussion about what to do to fix something. Talk openly about problems so that the whole team can work together to fix them – and so that everyone learns how to avoid them the next time.

Marano stresses giving increasing responsibility. "If they leave a book at home, don't run it over to the school. Let them feel what happens when they forget something. We're not talking about life and death here." The same holds true for the skills you want to help develop in your business. By permitting individual accountability, you make it clear that you want both your staff and your business to have the opportunity to 'grow up.'

CHAPTER 6

Don't Do Bad Business

Planning and Managing for Growth

As a child, Geoff always had to bounce off the same brick wall at least five times before he would finally realize that the wall wasn't going to move. Avery, on the other hand, watched Geoff bounce off the wall once, and it seemed to be enough for her to get the idea.

As they got older that difference showed itself most in their different approaches to planning.

For example, while they both generally had the same advance notice, and the same understanding of their school project schedule, Geoff would realize he needed project supplies about ten minutes after the stores had closed. It didn't seem to matter how many times we had the same problem. He had to take whatever folder or board he could buy at the 24 hour drug store.

> *Avery, on the other hand, being very specific about color or other specifications, planned her work so she would have what she would need.*
>
> *Eventually I stopped doing the 24 hour store program entirely. In the interest of my sanity, I kept a project materials supply on hand, and if they didn't plan ahead they had to choose from what was available. To date, I'm not sure that I took the best approach for helping Geoff get to more 'grown up' planning skills. On the other hand, he seemed to get the job done.*
>
> *Now that Geoff's driving and paying for his own gas to go to the 24 hour store, he seems to have figured it out. I guess gas money is a better motivator than the color of the folder. Once his lack of planning cost him gas money, he started thinking ahead.*

When is lack of planning just lack of the right motivator ? Maybe Avery planned ahead and carefully as her way to control the aesthetics of her project assignments. Once we were talking gas money, Geoff started to pay more attention.

Most people have some inherent ability to plan. The differentiator is how much training and experience they get, their motivation to be successful, and what level of discipline they apply. Where your plans are critical to growth, planning is critical.

> *"Plans are useless, but planning is indispensable."*
> —(President Dwight D. Eisenhower)

In the book *The Adaptive Enterprise; Creating and Leading Sense and Respond Organizations*, Stephan H. Haeckel talks about the challenge of planning for today's fast changing business environment. "The challenge is to make better sense out of the situation than the next guy."[13]

Avery watched her brother, and decided that having the exact supplies she wanted was important to her. She used planning ahead to control the outcome.

For a growing business, you need to be deliberate in deciding what's important for growth. Then you can plan accordingly.

The Three Little Pigs – What Will Get Your House Blown Down

We read kids the story of the three little pigs—one of Aesop's lovely life lessons disguised as politically incorrect stories for youngsters. The heart of the issue for the little piggies was the need to plan ahead in their choice of construction material, or risk their house being blown down.

The same kind of principles apply when you're planning for business growth. There are three critical things that can make, or break, the success of your plan.

- Tangible things that impact your ability to make decisions,

- Financial factors that can limit your rate and pace of growth, and

- Environmental considerations that guide where and how growth will be achieved.

Grown up companies avoid doing 'bad business' by staying focused on all three factors.

1. **Tangible things that impact your ability to make decisions.** These are the traditional considerations of people, space and technology. If you have no more office space, you can't add twenty new employees.

   As children grow up, we introduce them to planning by giving them an allowance. We orchestrate decisions that they can control. By forcing our teenagers to plan ahead for movies, they usually learn to pay attention to where their money actually goes.

   As a company 'grows up,' there's value in permitting the same kind of responsibility. That doesn't mean an open checkbook on expenses, but it also doesn't mean micro managing tradeoffs. Even in the smallest company, expect a discipline of what money will be spent on, how much it will be. Budget discussions should focus on the gaps between the expected spending and the actual spending. Focus your team on understanding and explaining the gaps, and look for the right level of decision making, ownership and accountability in those explanations.

   Look for the opportunities to let the day to day operational activities be managed by the people closest to them. Then hold them accountable.

   When I was the CIO at IBM, we were making a lot of changes to how we managed IT. Most of the costs I managed were budgeted on a per employee basis. Although my overall headcount to support was planned for a 20% + increase, I didn't get a 20% + budget increase. It was my job to figure out how to do it cheaper.

   I had the advantage of lots of proactive planning on how to leverage new technology. For example, instead of a big supplies budget for computer discs, we added software that used the network to share files. We spent a bit more than was budgeted for software, the wireless security functions and for training, but our supplies budget was almost completely unspent. I could bridge the gap and show the deliberate decisions that made the whole program cost less.

Senior executives need to look at plans and budgets in the context of planned growth. If you plan to add staff, or integrate an acquired company into the same physical space, do you have enough space and the right tools available? You won't want to cut off a hiring initiative because you have no desks left for the new people. Are you willing to look at flexible work arrangements? Those decisions need to be understood at an Executive level, as part of the growth plan.

There are also, however, things that should be managed at the level in the business where they can be planned and influenced. Then the effective executive can spend less time on specific line items and more understanding the levers that the team is using to manage cost. It's those levers that affect the growth and investment decisions.

2. **Financial factors that limit rate and pace of growth.** Depending on your business, rapid growth can have an impact on your operating line of credit or other critical management processes.

Take the teenager's allowance discussion. In a traditional world of high school dates, a teenage boy quickly learns that his allowance affords fewer trips to the movies when he starts paying for his date as well. Then he has three options:

- Rent movies to still have the date but spend less money.

- Start looking for ways to earn more money.

- Look for dates who are willing to pay their own way.

Many companies engage in a 'loss leader' strategy – the business equivalent of rented movie dates. In that case, it's critical to make sure that the boundaries and assumptions are well understood. Watching a rental movie at home has the added challenge of kid brother wanting to sit with you.

The second date option—earning more money so that you can pay for more dates—may be gratifying at the time, but it is only a sustainable approach if dating is all you ever want to do. At some point, the work time cuts into the fun time and the whole program falls apart.

Most companies need to look at option 3 – developing the kind of relationship that lets you split the cost of the outing. In a business context, it means working with your customers to have the deal be good for both of you.

Make sure that you understand the levers you have. Then you can effectively control and adjust the business model to accurately reflect impact.

3. **Environmental considerations that address where, and how, growth should be achieved.**

As a successful business, you may suddenly have the opportunity to buy other companies or take a more important building location with a sign at the street.

It's the business equivalent of the toddler looking at the treats in the candy store window.

Successful and manageable growth comes from deciding which deals to take.

When Lou Gerstner took over IBM, many of the businesses they owned were unrelated to computers or technology of any sort. In his book, Who Says Elephants Can't Dance, *Lou refers to divesting IBM of these distractions as an effort to 'stop the bleeding.' Although initially positioned as an expense reduction initiative, IBM didn't stop selling things off, even after Lou's initial target had been achieved. "As the years went by, we continued to streamline the business for other reasons."* [14]

I personally recall the angst and frustration that came from selling off the IBM owned golf courses and conference facilities. There was almost a personal sense of entitlement among the long term senior people. Lou's challenge was that golf courses and conference centers had nothing to do with selling computers, software or services. IBM could always rent a conference center, but as cash became tighter the distraction of running unrelated businesses wasn't worth the cost.

In his book *Profit From the Core,* Chris Zook talks about a clear definition of a company's core business as the foundation of sustained, profitable growth.[15] In North America, the highest success rates for mergers and acquisitions were found in small acquisitions made in related fields. What do you want to be different as a result of the acquisition program? What's your definition of success – Increased capacity? Talent? New offerings? New customers? Value to the shareholder?

Be sure to have clarity on the objectives so that you take the right growth strategy to address your top priorities for growth.

> *"Perspective is everything. For a worm, digging in the ground is more relaxing than going fishing."*
>
> —Clyde Abel

It takes a lot of discipline and business maturity to keep the focus on the right and logical places for growth. Lots of 'great deals' will go by. Being 'grown up' comes in avoiding distractions and having the perspective to know where your business' disciplines are, and where they're not.

In *A Nation of Wimps*, Marano encourages a parent to focus on the effort kids make. She says that "kids praised for their intelligence, rather than their effort, care more about grades than about learning. If you praise their intelligence and they fail, they think they aren't smart anymore… But kids praised for effort get energized in the face of difficulty."[16]

None of us will ever be perfect on planning. There will always be surprises. If what you want is a team of people who are competent in planning, keep the focus on the effort that goes into it. Recognize the discipline that supports the work. You may need to reward a good recovery, made possible by having the right thought in the plan, almost as much as you would have rewarded the initial plan's success. Reward the right trade-offs. As you 'grow up,' value the ability to adjust for the variances as much as you value the prevention of them.

CHAPTER SEVEN

Be Hard on the Problem, Not the People

People Strategies

Having been well warned about the challenge of teenagers, I started early planning little things that I do with each of my kids as sort of a little hook. If they ever went off to that gnarly teenager planet I had heard so much about, I might be able to have a link back to the smaller person who actually engaged.

With Avery, the hook is going downtown for a hair cut and some shopping. With Geoff, it's sitting down for dinner together. Lots of families do this every day, I realize, but between work and school, Geoff and Avery and I don't always eat dinner together.

> *I've found that if one of my kids seems a*
> *bit distracted or stressed about something, I can*
> *jump in to my mommy persona and either plan*
> *a haircut day or lay on a meal. Even if one*
> *of them is in gnarly teenager mode and being*
> *generally uncommunicative or hostile, they*
> *usually go along.*
>
> *I take a stab at topics to start a conversation,*
> *but I don't demand that they engage. Sometimes*
> *they have little to say, and sometimes they're the*
> *ones who start talking. Eventually though, if I*
> *make myself available, I can sort out if there is*
> *a specific issue or if they are just being teenagers.*
> *The most important thing is that they trust me*
> *not to press, so they feel safe to join in.*

Most parents work hard to have strategies that they can fall back on. Shopping trips, dinner together, vacations, taking the kids to ball games or dance classes. They all provide a safe environment, that isn't too intense, to have some quality time and contact. The trick is in both what you do and how you do it.

How many times have you watched parents at the arena or dance school? Great to make the effort to have the kids do skating. As adults, we remember 'what' we did—it clearly carries a lot of emotional weight.

The 'how' part of the outing, on the other hand, may be undermining the effort by not showing respect for each other's effort. Mom's been working all day, hasn't had dinner yet, and just really wants to get home and put her feet up – and it shows in the tugging and pulling and frustration with the kids. We all have crabby parent days – too many demands, too little time or money. Most kids figure out the telltale signs of a crabby day, and learn to stay clear when they see them. Bosses have crabby days too, but if we have people strategies in place that look at both what we do, and how we do it, a solid foundation in 'what you do' can carry you through.

Apply the same principles in business. Look at both what you do, and how you do it. As with kids, 'what' you do can produce loyalty and commitment, but how you do things indicates respect.

It's Amazing What You Can Get Done, If you're Prepared Not to Take the Credit – 'What' You Do

A big part of 'what' you do is both where and how you apportion blame or credit. If 'what' you do lets your staff feel supported and recognized, you're well positioned to get the loyalty and effort that you need. 'What' your company does will dictate how people feel coming in to work every day. People who start out the day with a smile will usually do more for their company than people who don't.

Think about the 'what you do' question both in terms of what recognition or feedback you give, and what kind of recognition the employee most values.

What recognition do you give?

Recognition can be either positive or negative. Feedback can be either acknowledgement or meant to help employees improve. In either case, people value honesty but they also expect genuine consideration of their feelings. What you do on a day to day basis can send lots of messages that you don't realize.

As with a parent's 'hooks,' your people strategies help you avoid potential problems by forcing the team to take a specific and consistent approach. There's a lot to be said for waiting for the right time and place to raise an issue.

In his book *The Secrets of Discipline*, Morrish emphasizes that "respect is a two way street. If you disregard their rights and needs, it's going to be difficult to teach your children to respect others."[17] In a business environment, regardless of size or age, it is just as critical to recognize the importance of the people you are counting on every day. Few of us can do everything alone.

> *"Life is like the car pool lane. The way to get to your destination quickly is to take some other people with you."*
>
> —Peter Ward

Think about 'what' your company does to be consistent and fair, and you'll have the loyalty and commitment you need to manage.

What kind of recognition is valued?

It's equally important to understand what motivates an employee – what do they value. For some people being recognized in front of their team mates is as important as a raise or a bonus. Some people would rather you invest in training and development. Don't assume it's about salary or bonus.

If you try to recognize a shy and introverted young employee by making them come up on a stage in front of dozens of clients and other employees, you may cause them discomfort more than making them feel good. That person may appreciate a quiet acknowledgement more.

If your people strategies encourage managers to understand what will truly motivate, instead of assuming their employees are all the same, you can get a lot more leverage from your investment and effort. You can also be much more tactical with key employees.

Most of us have personal or emotional reasons why we chose to work for one company over another. Work location flexibility is, for example, an important new currency in many cities. For some people, working from home a couple of days a week will be of more value than a bigger raise.

You can take this 'what' to do even further. What if you have a solid performer who's a little frustrated – a deal's not closing quite as fast as they hoped. Find something to recognize them for, even if you have to actually work with them proactively to make it happen. Create a recognition opportunity. That little boost can get them over the short term challenge so they keep on moving forward.

The 'what' you do is the family equivalent of taking the kids to hockey or skating. They can be regularly scheduled activities or a one-off, but they are the things that keep you on an even keel. If you do 'what' you should consistently, it will get you through rough water if the 'how' is sometimes not quite perfect.

We're All Doing the Best We Can – 'How' You Do It

We've all seen the mom or dad who's a bit crabby having rushed home from work to get the kids fed and then get off to skating—we're all human. 'How' we work together on a day to day basis won't always be perfect, but if we can respect the fact that we're all doing the best we can, the respect takes us a long way.

Younger children will often feel badly on a crabby day because they think that mommy is mad at them – she's not, she's just fatigued. As a parent, in the heat of the moment, it's easy to lose sight of the trust and security impact that a crabby day has.

Even in a grown up business, you need to make sure that your employees feel trust and security, or the insecurity will become a distraction for them and the people they work with. The book *Empowered Teams* emphasizes the importance of the team "having faith in each other, supporting each other, and generally behaving in a consistent and predictably acceptable fashion."[18]

Organizations "lose sight of the fact that teams are both business entities and social groups. There is a family-like nature to a team—for five days a week and eight or more hours a day. Unlike families, however, teams have diverse attitudes, values and backgrounds—that makes it even more important, but it also takes more effort, for the business groups to invest the time and effort to work together.[19] For a young business, where it is easy to think 'mommy's mad' instead of taking the day to day pressures in context, a solid team is critical to get past some of the crabby days.

Not unlike children, people who work together notice if others aren't getting along. They may avoid the friction, or deflect problems so that they don't get involved. Adults, unfortunately, have a longer memory. We have opinions and we talk about them. We take sides. We don't always start from the assumption that everyone is doing the best that they can with what they've got – In the moment you're probably getting the best they've got to give.

How often do we take the time to put someone else's crabby day in context ? How often do we have enough faith to try to understand the problem – maybe try to help. Trust is a two way street, and many of the business problems we have to handle every day could have been averted if there was enough mutual trust and respect to ask for help.

You're the Boss – Take Ownership

If you're the boss in a small company, you probably know almost everyone. You have the privilege of being close to every detail. That makes it easy to get close to problems, and it makes 'stepping in to help' seem like the right thing to do. For 'what' your company does and 'how' to do it, you're the most critical cog in the wheel. It's your job to encourage teamwork, trust and respect.

As soon as a parent gets conflicting stories on a problem, they know that they have to stop and figure out what's really going on. Some kids will take the blame for the broken lamp, because they know that their parent will be less strict if they own up fast. Some kids will never come clean, because deflecting is a strategy that's worked in the past.

None of us wants to have to be the parent, but if you are going to step into the team and start directing activities or decisions you have to take responsibility for the impact you have.

Give yourself the benefit of people strategies that force consistency and recognize the value of the team. Then on the days when the 'how' part of what making things happen isn't the smoothest, the 'what' part gives you the foundation of trust to keep on moving.

In his article "Staffing can cost you in more ways than one," published in the *Medical Post* (2003) Doug Payne writes "Hiring a new employee costs an average of $1,580. To terminate and replace that employee costs an average of $68,112." Many small businesses seem to want to solve problems by changing the players. If Payne is right, that's an expensive strategy. Your people strategy needs to give hiring, training, and re-training as much emphasis as it gives sales and other critical activities.

In *A Nation of Wimps*, Marano talks about 'what parents can do for their kids.' One point she makes is to "eat dinner together." Not just as a ploy, the way I do to give my son a chance to be heard, but as a critical socialization approach. "Eating dinner together makes children feel valued, loved and secure. It bolsters their sense of self. It's where they absorb values and information effortlessly... this is how the desire to be an effective adult is sustained."[20]

How do your employees absorb values and information? Look at what your company does to make sure that the people you are counting on feel valued and respected. Make sure that you have the programs in place to be fact based about who your key people are. Look for ways to make sure that everyone's efforts are appreciated and respected.

CHAPTER EIGHT

Think Twice, Talk Once

Communication

*One day Avery had finished work late and called
me for a ride. I was at a Board meeting and I
couldn't pick her up.*

*She was tired. She had worked a long day. It
was raining, so she was going to get wet. Things
just weren't good.*

*She did not want to hear that I was
unavailable. Nothing other than me saying
"I'm on my way" was the right answer, but
that couldn't happen. Her options were to get
a ride with my mother (otherwise known as
Grandmother), or take the bus even though it
was a bit late for her to be alone. Avery was
determined to have an attitude, so she was
planning to take the bus.*

*I called Geoff, and expressed my concern
about safety. He wasn't home to go and get her,*

73

> *but agreed that Avery should accept a ride with*
> *Grandmother for the sake of the safety. He called*
> *Avery and delivered that message as his own.*
> *Avery got a ride instead of taking the bus.*

Sometimes 'effective' communication isn't just about how you say things or what's said. Sometimes it's about who says it. Sometimes it's about what's said. Avery didn't want to listen to me, because at that exact moment she was not happy with me – so I got help from her big brother. She didn't want to hear what I had to say, but the same message – "Avery, this is a smarter idea"—was perfectly acceptable coming from Geoff.

With kids, we do whatever works. In business it is a bigger challenge to find the right combination of (1) how to say things, (2) what to say, and (3) who should say them. The communication tricks that parents use are also quick and easy guides in business.

There is no I in Team – How You Say Things

> *One Sunday I went into the laundry room to*
> *find a huge mound on top of the washer and*
> *dryer. Some things were dirty and had been*
> *on the floor waiting for a load earlier in the*
> *week. I had seen some of the items clean in the*
> *dryer after the cleaning lady's most recent visit.*
> *Now it was all mashed in together in a pile, so*
> *everything would need to be re-done.*
>
> *Easy as it would have been to wake Geoff*
> *and Avery up and make them come down and*
> *fix the problem, I just waited until they appeared*
> *for breakfast. Tempted as I was to start right in*
> *on the problem, I simply said "so, tell me about*

the big mound of clean and dirty laundry mixed up on top of the washer and dryer...." "It was dirty ?," said Avery. Then I got the whole story, and she went upstairs to fix the problem. Had I started out being angry or critical, we would have wasted a whole bunch of time on who did what and why. With me starting out neutral, she didn't need to engage defensively.

You can sometimes get a better result by thinking as much about how things are said as what is said. Use open probes instead of closed questions. Only use critical language if that is really what you mean to convey. Tone of voice and volume can significantly change the way a message is heard.

Stop and Breathe – What's Said

One of Avery's first boyfriends was a nice seeming fellow named Kevin. For the first few weeks I heard about 'her friend Kevin' as one of many. The request to go for an ice cream in the evening – just the two of them—seemed more like a date, so I said that Kevin had to come to the door and collect her properly. That was fine, and I went about my usual evening chores. Before Kevin arrived, Avery came back and said "now, you need to know that Geoff doesn't like Kevin that much. I just don't want him to say something that would be a surprise."

Hmmm. "Why doesn't he like him?," I ask. "Well, he's not part of his crowd, and he's a football player, and he's older." Hmmm. "How much older?," I say. Entertaining as this whole conversation was, the most important thing was

*that Avery clearly understood to get to me ahead
of Geoff, or risk having a different spin put on
the situation by her brother.*

*I did get the different spin from her brother,
but I was ready for it. I also did what any self
respecting parent does and checked with other
parents who knew him. They all said he was a
nice boy. I could move on.*

Everybody's got an opinion and everybody's heard a
rumor. It takes a lot of business maturity to stop and breathe
long enough to put things in context.

> *"A closed mouth gathers no foot"*
>
> —Steve Post

How often have you had to waste time hauling people
back from some rumor ? How often have you been distracted
by mis-interpretation of a meeting from people who weren't in
the room. How often have you been in a meeting that circled
around the real decisions to be made while everyone postured
and opined on vaguely related topics? How often have you
personally participated in these dust storms?

I frequently see otherwise calm and mature
professionals all hyped up about some little zinger they've
collected in the corridor. My usual tactic is to offer a bottle
of water to drink. I do that to force them to pause and think
about what they are saying. I often actually say "stop and
breathe." Then I ask a few questions.

"Start at the beginning – what are we talking about?"
(Always a good way to start.)

"Who has been involved already?" (Individual credibility and closeness to the real facts helps quickly assess the efficacy of the stories.)

"So what is the issue?" (Usually by now they have calmed down, and can get to the heart of the concern.)

Taking a stop and breathe approach with one person is easy. The actual questions don't matter. What you are really doing is creating cause to pause. If there actually is an issue, you can come from a position of calm to figure out a strategy. Most of the time, you'll already be aware of the situation and there are facts that the concerned person doesn't know. You can provide some context for the issue and assurance that the world is not coming to an end. Then the person can go back to a productive activity. Occasionally there will be an issue that you were not aware of, and by calming the person down enough to get to the facts and the sources you can quickly move to what to do.

The same kind of hysteria in a group setting is more of a feeding frenzy. The group dynamics often add a level of disrespect to the problem, with people talking over each other or generally just not listening. In his book *Recreating the Workplace*, Steven Raynor [21] gives the example of a company where the problem was addressed by having meetings attended by a small stuffed shark named Jaws. Whoever has Jaws in their hand has the right to speak and be heard.

As the boss, you need to be vigilant in your expectations of grown up communications. Listen for people regularly talking over others. If people have to say things like 'let me finish,' you have a problem. If you find meetings regularly regress, take a specific action like Jaws to force discipline and respect.

Deliberately Plan to Over Communicate – Who Says What

In my story at the start of the chapter, I could easily have just told Avery that Grandmother would pick her up – and she would have gone along with it based on my authority as the parent. Unfortunately, I knew that if I forced the answer, Grandmother would bear the brunt of Avery's frustration, which wasn't fair.

It is critical to understand the difference between what's meant to happen (the organization chart), and what actually happens (the 'social' organization). If you understand your company's social organization, you can use it to be more effective.

IBM's 1997 Worldwide study of 'The Role of the CIO in Business Transformation' identified effectively leveraged informal communication networks as one of the most significant contributors to sustainable change. Ronan McGrath, CIO of study participant CN, was recognized for having effectively harnessed the power of the informal network. Speaking to the broadly based 'communication mapping' in the CN study results, McGrath emphasized "you have to deliberately plan to over-communicate."

Every group of kids has one or two key leaders. We often seek out the oldest kid in a group and emphasize their age and trustworthiness as a preface to asking them to keep an eye out for the little ones. In business you can also know who the leaders are to effectively but informally get the right message into the group.

The key communicators in your social organization carry a lot of power – on both the right messages and the wrong messages. By understanding the social organization as part of your strategy for who communicates, you can build natural reinforcement. By sending the right messages into the informal network, you effectively cut off the dysfunctional communication that might occur otherwise.

Managing 'who' delivers the message can also effectively change the power positions. Think of the kid brother who never gets acknowledged by the big brother's group. Send him out with cookies and he'll suddenly have all kinds of attention – perhaps briefly, but quite effectively all the same.

Your company's social network will evolve naturally, but if you acknowledge that it exists and understand who the power communicators are, you can take advantage of it as a powerful tool. On important issues, pick a few well positioned people, and make sure that they have access to the facts. Make sure that the power communicators are not getting conflicting facts or confused messages – nature fills a void! Look for ways to bring them in to the planning on communication events that are important to your success.

A grown up company leverages both the informal and the formal communication channels, and gives people a chance to say what is on their mind in the right forum. Work on building a clear line of sight to whom you can count on to be respectful, relevant and fact based – they can help as communication role models for the rest of the organization.

As much as you may not want to be in the parent role, the most effective communication role model in your business is you. Many of us work in business environments where thinking about how and what we communicate is not a priority. We tolerate daily feeding frenzies. Pay attention to how and what people communicate. Identify the people you can trust. Make communication – what is said, by whom, and how – a 'growing up' priority. You'll make better decisions and you'll waste less time.

CHAPTER NINE

Know What You Don't Know

Decision Making

*In the spring of 2008, Geoff got his first car.
Then the cost of gas started going up.*

*"I think we need to find a car that's better
on gas. It's costing me a small fortune just to get
to and from the golf course."*

*"Now you understand why I used to ask you
to plan the route for collecting your friends when
I was doing the driving. That short haul, stop
and go stuff is pretty hard on the fuel tank." Not
a lot of sympathy on my side of the conversation.
On the other hand, Geoff is the guy who has to
bounce off the wall a few times before he'll accept
that he isn't going to get through it. This is going
to be a truly painful and ongoing debate unless
he figures it out for himself.*

"So, what are you thinking of?" I say.

"Well, the hybrids like the Prius seem to be pretty well rated." Right, I think, have you ever gone and looked at a Prius? Geeky car if I ever saw one.

"OK, so maybe you should go and drive one of those and see what you think." The look on his face made it very clear that he didn't expect me to go along quite this much. "By myself?" he said.

"I can call the dealership and tell them I need them to help you. If I make the call I'm sure that they'll give you a test drive. Then, if we need to, we can go back. While you're at it, maybe go check out really small cars, like the Mini Cooper." I knew people who had bought Mini's, and they're kind of uncomfortable, so I knew the cool factor wouldn't last once he drove it.

Geoff was a man on a mission. I spent the next few weeks listening to his debrief on what he had learned that day about the options. I will admit, he did a good job of lining up all the tradeoffs.

Eventually we got to the discussion of what's actually involved in trading a car. Factor number one was what his car would get on a trade-in. My very helpful used car dealer asked Geoff a few well crafted questions (he'd obviously had this problem before…). "How much do you drive in a month?" Geoff learned that unless he was driving a lot of distance all the time, the payback period was well over 5 years. Hmmm. "What about the fact that you have a full parts and labor warranty – you won't get that back

*on a trade-in." Then the close… "So, I can give
you the top book price for this car, which gets you
what you need for the Prius. Then you'll need
to write a cheque for the taxes—that's about
$3,000." That's a lot of gas. Geoff was pretty
silent all the way home.*

*That night he talked about the next
generation of hybrids, which would probably
have the kinks worked out about the time he
finished University. He told me that his car really
was at the better end of middle of the road for
mileage. He wouldn't have wanted to leave his
new stereo system in the car if it was traded in,
and he didn't really like the look of the Prius.
Maybe he'd just drive this one through University
– then worry about it.*

*I did all that I could to reinforce how
impressed I was with his analysis, and support
his decision on the matter as a wise one indeed.
He went away happy.*

One bullet dodged. I needed Geoff to be committed
to the end result, so he needed to manage the decision making
process. When he started, he was pretty certain that he had
most of the facts. I knew a few things that maybe he didn't, but
I also gave him credit for having more interest in cars than I do.
Maybe there was something I didn't know. While I was hoping
I knew where the decision would come out, he needed to have
the opportunity to get there in his own way.

Young children will respond reasonably well to
direction. Most of us know that the way to end a visit at the
park is not to ask "so, are you ready to go?" unless you're

prepared to stay there all day. You have to be directive – "time to go home."

You can plan your approach to decision making by thinking through the path to a sensible decision to get the most mature response.

> *"Common sense is not so common"*
>
> —Voltaire

Common sense is an important sign of maturity for your company, and you'll see it demonstrated (or not) in how your team approaches decision making.

A child who doesn't have all the information she needs will generally just avoid or delay deciding anything. They want to know exactly who is going to be at the BBQ before they decide whether to come along or stay home with the sitter. Where you need to make a decision based on incomplete information, an adult will make the best decision that they can, understand the trade-offs being made, and then adjust as they go in the execution.

Rocks, Paper, Scissors—How to Make a Decision

Kids have lots of games that are set up to make decisions – the outcome doesn't really matter. As adults the outcome usually does matter, so we have to be willing to ask questions and take advice. If you know how to bring together the right information, you can engineer 'common sense.'

Most people start a business, or take a job, based on what they know. But how well do we actually <u>know</u> what we know?

For example, you're a sales person. You've gone into business because you find a great product that fills a real void. You're the person to sell it. *You know what you know.* Knowing what you know gives you commitment.

The second critical element in making a decision is to *know what you don't know.* You may know how to make and sell the product, but do you know what it takes to ship and invoice? If not, you need to take the lesson from Bill Gates—invest in the person who can set up and manage that side of the business, to make sure that you can fulfill the orders. Knowing what you don't know lets you get the answers you need to be successful.

The third possibility to consider is that you *don't know what you don't know.* In that case, you have two options: (1) try to keep every decision outcome within your influence or control so that you can adjust for what you didn't know, or (2) always assume that there will be things you don't know. Option two lets you stay open to those around you. Accepting that you may not know what you don't know prevents surprises.

Finally, you may even find that you <u>didn't know that you knew.</u> Perhaps you were just reminded by the person you listened to and trusted. Being open to recognize that you didn't know what you knew gives the whole team the confidence to go forward.

By recognizing the 'know' and the 'don't know' side of the decision making process, you engineer common sense by asking questions. Enable your whole team to ask the questions that will help them to both make and manage the decision.

	Know	Don't Know
Know	*I Know What I Know (KWK) –* Make the decision	*I Don't Know What I Know (DKWK)* – Ask questions of the people you think DO know; Unless you can move to KWK, take their advice
Don't Know	*I Know What I Don't Know (KWDK) –* Delegate to, or ask questions of, the people you think do know	*I Don't Know What I Don't Know(DKWDK)* – Get the team together and let them educate you; Learn from the interaction as much as the individuals

Figure 9.1 How to Make an Informed Decision

Lead by example. Make it ok to ask questions, and to say 'I don't know.' Engage your staff in active discussion about what might not be known or obvious. Treat any unanswered question as a 'don't know,' making it penalty-free to go looking for the person who can help.

Maybe Mom Won't Catch Us—Taking Risks

The good news in my Geoff and the car story is that he ultimately made the same decision that I would have on my own. What if he had found a really economical car that he actually did like? If I was not committed to potentially changing cars, I took quite a risk.

Although Geoff couldn't make a decision without me, I really was open to there being things that I didn't know. If he really could find enough information to convince me, then we would have had some other decisions to make. Even though I was not expecting it, (and I was hoping it would not be the case), if there was a different decision that should be made I was open to it.

My risk mitigation strategy was to steer him to get fact based on the things that he didn't know, and then to trust his ability to use common sense.

Kids take risks all the time. Sneaking that extra cookie, taking the risk that mom won't notice. Sneaking next door to see a friend's new toy, even though dad said "stay in the yard." A group of teenagers trying to get into a PG rated movie, even though some might get turned away. These risks seem safe, because they either don't expect to get caught, or if they do the consequences don't mean that much to them. Mom will laugh and say "you don't get dessert after dinner" It was just going to be a cookie, so no real difference.... The teenagers won't get to see the movie, but the odds are that if one gets stopped they'll all get stopped so they'll all still be together.

The difference for grown up decision making is that we realize the risks really can happen, and there is usually far more vested in the down side if they do. Every business has time when they must make decisions in spite of the risks. A grown up business understands what the risks are, and looks for ways to mitigate.

In his book *Taking Charge of Change,* Douglas K. Smith talks about risk taking in decision as a point of 'courage.' He gives examples of courage decisions we make in our work world every day—"to learn new skills… to collaborate with unfamiliar people … to take on added responsibilities."[22] Decisions take courage.

> *My daughter's summer job had a variable schedule, and she had volunteered to take the early start time each day. Her team mates preferred a later time and the early time was better for her on the train. After a week or so, she found herself again scheduled for the later start, and others had the early times. She needed to decide whether to take a bus and risk being late, or whether to take her usual train and be very early. She decided to take her usual train. At the risk of being seen as complaining, she decided to use her early arrival as the trigger for a conversation with her boss to re-state her preference for the early start. She mitigated the risk by using the time on the train to plan her communication.*
>
> *As it turns out, the supervisor had put her on a later start because she handled one part of the job better than the other students. Her decision to talk to her supervisor gave her the benefit of the positive feedback. It went so well that the supervisor was prepared to share the*

*risk with her, and said that if that she wanted
to try taking the later bus, and risk being a few
minutes late, that would be ok.*

Avery's supervisor was also a summer student, but he was 'grown up' in his approach to recognizing the options and making creative decisions. He saw an option that let him give Avery some valuable positive feedback, and reinforced it by making a decision to make his outcome easy for Avery. They shared the risk.

Organizational maturity comes in recognizing the decision point and options that are in front of us, and thinking it through before we actually pick one. Grown up businesses make informed decisions, and they understand and mitigate the risks.

If you know what the risks might be, you can truly understand the potential consequences of the decision. Then you can decide if you can accept those consequences. If you can't accept the potential consequences, you have another decision – change your mind, or take extra precautions to make sure that nothing goes wrong.

In *A Nation of Wimps*, Marano's advice for raising decisive children is to "encourage your kids to problem-solve and take risks."[23] She goes on to say "have high expectations… Then support your kids in creating their own paths to those expectations." She emphasizes encouraging them to look at as many perspectives as possible, and if they get stuck she suggests asking them questions to help – not taking over the decision for them.

One of the earliest steps in growing up is to learn to ask questions and then learn from the answers. Start with decision making as the place where you model the behavior—

give yourself permission to 'not know," and provide a safe environment for your employees to do the same.

CHAPTER TEN

Prepare the Child for the Path, Not the Path for the Child

Leadership

Geoff started golfing relatively late in kid golfer terms, so he was one of the older boys when he played his first junior tournaments. He signed up for a full summer event, where the boys gradually worked through a roster of one-on-one games to get to a junior club champion.

Geoff was near the top of the age category, and his first game was with a much younger fellow – a nice kid Geoff thought highly of, so he felt really badly going out on a win-or-lose basis. Geoff spent most of his time in the round finding ways to be supportive and positive with his young competitor. He did win the round, but his little buddy came out of the day feeling good about his effort and they were good friends for the rest of the summer.

Although Geoff wouldn't think to describe his behavior as leadership, that's what it was. He earned trust and confidence through the round, and turned a potentially unhappy situation into a good experience.

It is hard to define leadership. Common words that surround it include trust, respect, confidence and loyalty. It has something to do with that style or approach to people and efforts that gets results; inspiring instead of intimidating; creating and maintaining cooperation; gaining power through trust; encouraging change; bringing out the best in people. Some pretty ethereal and lofty objectives, but basically the same things we know work with kids.

Consider Sal Severe's 'Ten Principles to Practice' [24] from the book *How to Behave So Your Children Will Too*:

1. Pay off correct behavior, not misbehavior.

2. Think before you talk. Say what you mean. Mean what you say.

3. Expect good behavior.

4. Coach on ways to be successful.

5. Anticipate problems and set out the rules in advance.

6. Teach decision making and accountability.

7. Start early; be strict but positive.

8. Focus on positive qualities – teach to feel good about doing the right thing.

9. Support yourself. Be a good model.

10. Provide a healthy and pleasant climate. Talk about values and goals.

Severe's focus is on the things that toddlers and young children need as a base to build on. In my experience with smaller and younger companies, the needs are the same.

It's easy for the management of a small or young company to be directive. It goes with the need to wear many hats and just get the job done. Unfortunately, while it may get the 'management' job done it doesn't develop or enable leadership.

We all know people who think through everything for their kids, and direct every thought and decision. As a result, the kids become teenagers and they still don't know how to take responsibility for themselves – because they've never had to. Taking over the active and hands on management is a vicious circle—your staff don't have a chance to move away from needing day to day involvement to keep things moving forward.

Give Up The Baby Gates

When Avery was born, Geoff was only a year old. We lived in a house with a staircase that defied any sort of baby gate, so we put a great deal of effort into helping Geoff learn how to be safe and self sufficient with the stairs. He'd start on his hands and knees at the top, and back his little self up to the top step and then down one step at a time. We had a few spills, but by the time Avery came home from the hospital Geoff was perfectly able to accompany me up and down the stairs without any assistance. When Avery started to crawl, he proceeded to teach her exactly the same technique. Stairs were well understood by both of them, so I never really had to worry about them.

Then one day we had guests who visited bringing along their four year old. The mom had been ill, so as a safety measure they made liberal use of baby gates to keep the lttle one within range. Unfortunately I was so used to Geoff and Avery's skills with stairs that when we went out to the yard, which involved about three steps on the deck, I did not even think to offer instruction. The poor little mite went straight off the top step – fortunately the grass at the bottom buffered the landing, but it was quite a shock.

In business, leadership is the context that lets you know the kids won't go careening off the top step. It's the foundation that gives your organization the confidence to handle all the little day to day things that need to get done. It's the base of respect and support that keeps things together without you directing every step along the way.

> *"Your job gives you authority. Your behavior earns you respect."*
>
> —*Irwin Federman*

Children decide for themselves who they respect and trust. They naturally gravitate to people who are positive, supportive and inclusive. Employees are the same. Leadership creates an affinity based on trust and respect.

In his book *The Milkshake Moment*, Steven Little emphasizes that for organizations to grow they need "true leadership, not simply management." He builds an acronym based on the word TRUST[25] that has a lot in common with Severe's ten principles to practice:

- Timely

- Realistic

- Unscripted

- Sensitive

- Transparent

Timely – Successful growth leaders devote their time to those areas that truly need it – not just on the tasks that they are most comfortable completing. Leaders understand the nature of time and are skilled at prioritizing it to make an impact.

Realistic – What distinguishes growth leaders is their unrelenting focus on what really is and what truly can be. Growth leaders seek only the truth and welcome any and all reality checks.

Unscripted – What we long for is authenticity. We want leaders who speak plainly and from the heart. In order to lead it is critical to master the art of authenticity. Say what you mean and mean what you say.

Sensitive – Growth leaders are acutely aware of their surroundings and are keenly observant. They have an intuitive knack for understanding the motivations of others. They have the uncanny ability to gain insight from seemingly disparate data.

Transparent – People and organizations that are transparent in their actions come out ahead in the long run. Those who are forthcoming with information – good and bad – can more effectively lead a team to accomplish great things. Employees, customers, suppliers and shareholders know what to expect from transparent leaders.

The challenge of leadership may arguably be the toughest part of helping your business grow up. As the leader, you're being watched by people who want—and need—to know how to help. Every action you take, and every inaction you permit, is being sliced and diced – talked about and analyzed.

> *"Behavior you ignore is behavior you permit"*
>
> —Ronald G. Morish

Nature does a good job of filling a void. You have the option of giving your team the vision and context you want them to have, or they'll make one up and work with that. As with parenting, none of us will get it right every time. The respect and confidence that you attract, and the reality check that gets you through the occasional mistake, are based on you being seen to do what's right.

Kids need to see their parents make an effort – some days they seem to deliberately force us to go out of our way – mainly to test if we will. They challenge us constantly to see if our actions are consistent with what we tell them to do. That doesn't mean that they love us any less if we mess it up sometimes, but if they know that we are doing our best they'll usually step up and try to do the same. Your employees are no different. How you handle situations; your reactions in tough times; your willingness to admit an error – all go into your team's assessment of you as a leader. Let them see you striving to do what's right.

Don't Let 'em See You Sweat

As is the case with every large company, when I was at IBM I had one year where there was quite a bit of pressure at a leadership level on some planning challenges that were impacting our results. It was pretty intense for the senior team – but that's why they pay you the mediocre bucks. When I moved to a new role, the person who took over some part of my responsibilities was promoted from within the team that reported to me. We had lunch a month or so later to talk about how it was going, and the first thing she said to me was 'none of us had any idea what you were dealing with. You really buffered us from the reality.' I apologized for the surprise factor, but I did feel both pride and accomplishment in that I felt I had done the right leadership job.

As parents, we spend a lot of effort and energy trying to make sure that the kids feel safe and the world seems stable. The toughest part of having a sick child, or being ill as a parent, is that we have to play it down and not let the kids see our anxiety. They have no point of reference for it, and until there is a definitive answer on whatever the problem is they don't need to feel it.

The same goes for your business. Your employees don't need to know all the puts and takes that you deal with on a day to day basis, and it can be distracting and damaging if they do.

It is critically important that you demonstrate a sense of urgency at all times – absolutely. But they should not see the play by play on your anxieties or concerns.

By definition, a touchstone is "any test of genuineness or values."[26] Kids are constantly looking for touchstones as the base on which to launch their own actions and decisions. They derive a sense of connectedness, they get perspective and clarity, and they develop a level of inspiration and gratitude that helps them to stave off misplaced priorities as they go." The kids will grow up whether they have these foundational points of reference or not, but the effective establishment of these touchstones is a key contributor in what makes some parents more effective than others.

As parents we build little hooks like trips out for ice cream as a touchstone when we need it. Leadership is the touchstone that lets you keep your team going forward in the right direction without your having to direct every thought and action.

Businesses can grow without being focused on leadership, but leadership can be that touchstone that changes your focus from just growing to growing up.

Chapter Eleven

Crawling to Walking

The Toddler Years

*Young children, by definition, need guidance and
structure. We structure activities like summer
camps and play dates. We try to encourage
finishing with one game before bringing out three
others. Relationships are decided by who lives
next door and who the parents visit with. Life is
pretty much in the moment.*

Things are much the same for a small or young
company. It takes a lot of curiosity and energy just to keep the
momentum. Keeping the bank happy – like keeping the kids
safe – is a primary concern. The senior executives are involved
in the detail and making the decisions. This chapter explores
the specific things that will be helpful in a small or younger
company.

Debrah Lee Charatan, President of Bach Realty was
nearing $10 million in annual revenue when she realized

"for us to grow more, I had to stop selling. I found that my salespeople did not feel free to talk to me about their problems while they were competing with me. Some associates were afraid to ask for my assistance."[27] She needed to maintain the respect and trust, but instill some distance for her sales force to stand on it's own and be more effective.

At what stage does the "boss" need to step back from keeping the toddler safe – at what stage can they start to prepare the child for the path, instead of the path for the child? How to best do that? What is unique about a young child that impacts what you need to do – or not do – to help your organization grow up?

Contracts & Metrics

Your business may have little or no real experience with what disciplined measurements and contracts are. As do children, a small business will test the boundaries, so you need to be vigilant about being fact based.

There are three contract and metric considerations that will hold you back as you try to grow:

- Misunderstood data,
- Misaligned contracts, and
- Unrealistic goals

Misunderstood Data

Many young companies build measurements, contracts, and even compensation, on data that is not well understood. This leaves gaps in the collection process, it leads to things being missed, and it can result in different and confusing interpretations of the same information.

> *"Don't look at where you fell, but where you slipped."*
>
> —African Proverb

You end up asking questions like 'is this sales figure based on orders, or shipped and invoiced product?' 'Does the cost of an employee include the direct burden costs, like a computer and cell phone?' 'Are the year over year figures adjusted for that organization change that we made in March ?' Many young companies avoid using a lot of the data they have, because it is too difficult to anticipate and answer the questions that might arise.

Be prepared to learn where the data comes from and what's included or not. Try to avoid manual data unless it is produced through a well understood process. Make it 'penalty free' for people to ask questions and to not have all of the answers—be in learning mode on what the data is saying. The best strategy you can take is to improve everyone's knowledge gradually, so you can all understand the data better over time. As long as you don't have the same misunderstanding repeatedly, you're making progress.

Misaligned Contracts

Many young companies have different employee, client and supplier contracts for every situation. Employment letters will vary depending on the hiring manager. Most of the client and supplier contracts will have client or supplier driven terms.

There are three steps to take:

- Get baseline contracts and standard employment letters in place, so that you have a point in time at which you're consistent going forward.

- Do a gap analysis on your existing customer and supplier contracts. Prioritize the ones that are coming up for renewal, so you are prepared to negotiate to your baseline terms. Also look at the ones that have a very long life or a very high potential dollar value. Understand the gaps.

- Build a deliberate plan to renegotiate and re-sign contracts that are significantly offside with where you need to be.

You won't get all of your contracts re-aligned over night, but by understanding the gaps and tracking what is outstanding you're in a position to reduce your exposure and eventually get it cleaned up.

Unrealistic goals

This can be an issue both for setting business targets and for making business commitments.

In the book *I Hate to See a Manager Cry*, Martin R. Smith talks about unrealistic goals as a key indicator of a need to grow up. "Nothing reveals the immature personality as quickly as the tendency to set up unrealistic goals."[28] Without specific metrics that tell you how much a project costs or how long it takes, you will be more likely to commit things without knowing what you can deliver – 'I'll have that fixed today' … 'I'll look after it right away' … It's easy to get caught up in the moment, and you control the resources so brute force often gets the job done on time, but maturity lies in understanding and committing to what's possible instead of resorting to brute force.

Process

You may not have done much formal work on process. That doesn't mean you don't have any, it just isn't formalized or specifically invested in. Start by looking at what your people actually do – see what's really there. Build on that.

Don't fall in the 'spend money to save money' trap. The folly many businesses find themselves in is that they believe if they invest in formal and structured processes, it will reduce their operating costs in future years. It won't. It can protect you from mistakes. It can create a consistent jargon across your business. It can make it possible for you to grow more cost effectively. But it is not a cost take out exercise.

> *"Doing the right thing is always easier in practice than in theory."*
>
> —Steven S. Little

In her book *A Nation of Wimps*, Marano observes that the need for vigilance is "enormously taxing." She says "quit hovering over your kids."[29] Process that reduces your need for your personal vigilance is a good place to focus in your efforts to grow up.

When your company is small, and processes are simple, is also a good time to start to focus on quality. In the book *Quality is Free*, Philip B. Crosby emphasizes that quality may not be what you think it is. He goes on to say that "quality has much in common with sex. Everyone is for it (under certain conditions). Everyone feels that they understand it (even though they would not want to explain it). Everyone thinks that execution is only a matter of following natural instincts (after all, we do get along somehow). And, of course, most people feel that all the problems in this area are caused by other people (if only they would take the time to do things right)."[30]

Understand what outcomes you're after with the process. Task the team with defining both clear metrics and quality steps. If you start into key processes when you are small, you can keep it simple and get benefits in quality, metrics and overall business productivity.

Making Change

Young children are very aware of what they're allowed to do. The 'my mom won't let me' program is even sometimes used as an excuse to avoid doing something the kid actually doesn't want but they don't want to say so.

In the book *The Milkshake Moment*, Steven Little talks about this child-like behavior in the context of companies making change. He says that "organizations look for reasons why they can't do things."[31] Depending on the changes you want to see in your business, the natural child-like response of 'they won't let us' can be an easy avoidance tactic and difficult to overcome.

> *"Vision without execution is daydreaming."*
>
> —Bill Gates

Be very clear on what you want to be different and look for evidence that the change is being achieved. Start by defining the steps that you need to see for the change to happen. Discussion of the steps is not commitment, so take the steps one at a time and stick it out.

Planning and Managing for Growth

While a three year old spends much of his time worried about keeping Mommy happy, a young company's planning and growth management is probably about keeping the bank happy. In the book *Winner Take All*, Webster talks about the need to "earn and maintain support."[32] Having credibility to build supportive relationships is critically important, especially with bankers, investors, and your senior team.

For children, credibility comes from doing what is expected of them. If you expect them to be home by dinner time, most of the time they will. The challenge in having expectations is to make sure that the kids can be successful. Expecting a child to stay neat and clean all day probably doesn't also allow an expectation of having a good time playing with the other kids on the street. One expectation or the other is unlikely to be met.

In a business context, planning and managing for growth will also have mutually exclusive elements. For example, if you have a manager with day to day responsibilities that demand constant and detailed attention to the work of a large team, it is probably not realistic to expect her to also spend at least one full day a week at a client site. She will not be able to do both.

I think of it as juggling balls in the air when you have dogs biting at your ankles. You're either looking up to juggle and you'll get bit, or you're looking down to shoo the dogs and you'll drop the balls. Nothing is more frustrating than an objective that you know you can't meet. Make sure that your plan is built on what is do-able.

> *"The discontent of the people is more dangerous to a monarch than all the might of his enemies on the battlefield."*
>
> —Isabella d'Este

With a small company, and a small team, most of the senior people will have to multi-task. Make sure that what you expect of them can be done.

People Strategies

Think about young children's behavior in relationships. For example, kids make friends in the moment. The boy who made friends with a kid because he has a cool bike and shoes, and his own cell phone, may have a problem at home when he starts to want the same things. Parents are usually actively involved in selecting social situations and playmates who are compatible, to avoid problems later.

Young companies have the same challenge. You need to choose the right people to do what needs to be done. You may not have time to develop the talent, or work up to the experience that you need. If you're going to pay for a senior sales manager, that person needs to be able to hit the ground running. Your company may not, however, know how to make sure they pick the right person.

In the book *Thriving on Chaos*, Tom Peters focuses on having the key team mates involved in recruiting to make the right choices. He also says don't rush. "Spend time and lots of it. Insist that the line people dominate the process and don't waffle about the qualities that you are looking for."[33] By having the close working team involved, you demonstrate that the job being filled is important to you, and you make it clear that the people involved in the recruiting process have some responsibility for the person's success.

Assess not only the technical skills or the actual experience you need in senior roles—think ahead about the personality and leadership that you need as well. Peters goes on to say "only promote those people whose greatest pleasure is bragging about the accomplishments of their front line troops." Pay attention, in the interviews, to not only what they say but how they say it. Look for strong leadership attributes.[34]

Once you have hired the person, you have to figure out how to help them build the relationships that they need to be successful. Think of the eight year old who snubs her long time friend to be accepted in the cool crowd at school. Not many young children understand the importance of commitment and supportiveness in a relationship. The team members who participated in your recruitment and selection process carry the responsibility for then being proactive to help the new person settle in and be productive quickly.

> *"Men build too many walls and not enough bridges."*
>
> —Sir Isaac Newton

The people strategies you use to help a new employee get settled also work to keep your existing staff happy. It takes commitment to keep everyone focused on the job.

In *The 7 Habits of Highly Effective People*, Covey talks about the commitment bank. "Keeping a commitment or a promise is a major deposit; breaking one is a major withdrawal."[35] One of the most common mistakes that smaller and younger companies make is not building the relationship currency – not building up their commitment bank account – to make the team work effectively.

Grown ups know that relationships take work.

Communication

Children's communication is generally 'in the moment' – what they want now, and what's happening next. 'In the moment' communication is also in evidence in many small companies, so it takes extra focus and effort to keep communication in context.

In *Recreating the Workplace*, Rayner uses the term 'serendipity.' Serendipitous communication leverages "influence and timing rather than rationale and logic. Many decisions that have a direct impact are the result of chance encounters."[36]

Spontaneity is good, but it may not be the foundation for building your business. In the book *The Adaptive Enterprise*, Haeckel talks about commitments in terms of saying what you mean and meaning what you say.[37] He emphasizes the need to have all the right people involved in a discussion, even if that makes it more difficult. He talks about "who owes what to whom" as the foundation to ensure definition and acceptance. You need to avoid the kind of serendipitous communication that results in isolated decisions.

Think about who owes what to whom. If you have an 'executive team,' you need to be accountable to each other. Think about how the executives need to communicate and formalize the strategies that you need to keep focused on making your business grow.

Decision Making

After her son said 'I don't care,' the mom said 'that's ok dear, because I do. And that's why it's my choice. Some day, when you care about it as much as I do, it will become your choice.

Young children have a limited capacity for effective decision making both in terms of what they know and in terms of their personal experience to understand what's at stake. Many of the employees in a younger company have the same experience gap. The most significant risk is that, as a result, a traditional decision making process will be weighted toward the person with the best sales skills. In *The Adaptive Enterprise*, Haeckel talks about the traditional 'pitch' approach to making decisions – individuals or groups come in and present their ideas looking for decisions.[38] "The pitch is designed to sell the proposed solution to the decision makers. This advocacy process creates an adversarial culture, where the advocate intends to sell the proposal and the reviewers counter with the attitude 'buyer beware.'" The risk is that the less mature and less confident participants may be the ones with important information to contribute.

Getting to Yes looks at the negotiation aspect of the decision making process. "When negotiators bargain over positions, they tend to lock themselves in. The more you clarify and defend your position the more committed you become to it."[39] The risk is the same.

> *"Evil communications corrupt good manners."*
>
> —Bible

The impact of child-like behavior on your decision making process is significant. We've all seen what happens when dad has one opinion and mom has another—children will quickly learn to manipulate. The less mature your company, the more important it is to know what you know, and know what you don't, so you don't let yourself or your business be manipulated.

Leadership

The younger your company, the more you will feel as if you're in the parental role. Like parents, you will often feel that you need to be all things to all people.

Many of Severe's ten principles to practice[40] relate leadership oriented demands to the challenges of raising young children:

- "Pay off correct behavior

- Say what you mean; mean what you say

- Be clear what you expect from them and what they can expect from you

- Anticipate problems; provide support and encouragement

- Teach decision making and accountability"

Severe's principles really are the touchstones you need to give people as the leader.

"How does your dog miraculously know that you are going to take him for a walk? While you are watching him only 1 percent of the time, he watches you 99% of the time."[41] Your staff watch what you do, how you do it, and how it affects everything else.

David Novak, in *The Education of an Accidental CEO*, advises "think of yourself as a brand. Be aware of the kind of image you want to reflect."[42]

> *"A candle loses nothing of it's light when lighting another."*
>
> —Kahlil Gibran

In *Working With Emotional Intelligence,* Daniel Goleman talks about the amygdala—a little almond shaped gland at the base of your skull that is the source of gut feeling.[43] Everybody has one. The amygdala clicks in the instant something starts to feel emotional, and if you're the one doing the talking you have about 30 seconds while the person listening to you decides if everything is ok. With everyone watching you, and all the little amygdalae clicking in everywhere, you really need to be self aware.

> *In a recent management meeting, I was sitting across the table from a peer who you would quickly observe to be a very precise sort of fellow – work binder organized with tabs and different colors sizes of postie notes lined up neatly by size. As a result of some unfortunate shuffling of speaker phones from the end of the table, his carefully structured book became the unwitting victim of a full cup of coffee.*

> *In the confusion that ensured, everyone pitched in to sop up the mess and get the meeting back underway. Unfortunately my friend who's book had taken the hit was absolutely unable to focus for about 20 minutes.*

> *You could see the pain on his face – hear the voice in his head saying 'It's ruined. Ruined!' The emotional trigger was immediate and absolute – his amygdala had clicked in and he could not let go of the emotional response to come back into the meeting at hand.*

Goleman treats "accurate self assessment" as an emotional intelligence competence.[44] He emphasizes the need to "be aware of your strengths and weaknesses, be reflective and learn from experience, be open to candid feedback, and show a sense of humor about yourself."

Leadership is one of the toughest parts of your job, but like parenthood it can also be one of the most rewarding things you do.

In Hara Estroff Marano's book *A Nation of Wimps*, Marano talks about "the Executive portion of the brain... the circuitry of self regulation and attention."[45] A small business needs to develop that self regulation. Once you've identified your priority areas for more grown up behavior, put the effort in and get to the next level.

The early years are the foundation to be well behaved and decisive. They position you to become a teenager.

CHAPTER TWELVE

The Age of Reason

The Teenage Years

*An adolescent is essentially ready to grow up –
they just need to be pushed along to actually do
it. Now's the time to push the maturity bar to
where you ultimately want it to be.*

*Maturity will be personal, and your focus
needs to be on 'hearts and minds one at a
time.' You can't just send the kid off on a bus
to summer camp anymore – they're home alone
while you go off to work. You have to trust them
– both their own judgment and that of their
friends.*

In *How to Behave So Your Children Will Too*, Severe says
"attempts to control teenagers are futile. You must depend on
your teenagers to cooperate with your ideas of right and wrong.
You must count on them to make their own decisions."[46]

Youth is both creative and oblivious. This is the time to invest in independence but keep control of the curfew. Time to invest in the general maturity that your company needs and in the management development that makes it sustainable. In *The Secrets of Discipline*, Morrish emphasizes that "independence isn't doing your own thing, it's doing the right thing on your own."[47]

Now is the time to decide to be grown up.

Contracts & Metrics

Adolescents are learning from experience. They're trying different ways to get what they want and need. They're testing the boundaries. They're building their own set of 'rules' for how the world around them operates. Your company is doing the same – building it's own set of business rules to frame the way you work and the decisions you have to make.

For example, when Microsoft first started, Frank Gaudette made the decision to carry no book value for software. Assets like Windows and Microsoft Office, which could have been depreciated over time, were treated as valueless. Microsoft's stock consistency and strength can be attributed to that accounting decision.

Contracts and metrics support you by making sure that the business rules are fact based. They help you make sure that you're able to measure your progress, and that you're able to anticipate the things that can affect your ability to grow.

> *"Get the facts first. Then you can distort them as much as you please."*
>
> —Mark Twain

At this stage in your development, you're using financial data to understand and manage your business with integrity, and exercising deliberate control through your contracts. The final dimension in becoming an adult is to 'measure beyond money.'

In his book *The Milkshake Moment*, Little suggests that "ultimately profit and loss statements aren't enough to get even accountants out of bed."[48] Start to think through and measure everything that's integral to your growth strategies – cycle times, defect rates, exceptions to the process (if you aren't already). Keep in mind that data isn't information. It takes a collection of data, brought together with insight and knowledge of the business, to draw conclusions. As a teenage company, you need to start to move from reporting data to looking at information.

In *Thriving on Chaos*, Peters sets out six rules for effective use of data.[49] He emphasizes "measuring what's important":

1. **Simplicity of presentation** – Your reporting should be like a dashboard. When you look at the dashboard on your car, you can see all of the critical things – speed, temperature, engine performance and fuel levels. If you look at cars like the BMW M6, intended for very high speeds, they go so far as to reflect the critical dashboard indicators like speed and RPM's in the driver's vision on the windshield. At the speeds the M6 is intended to do, they want the driver to see what they need but still keep their eyes on the road.

2. **Visibility of measurement** – If measurements have to be vetted before they can be distributed, there's something wrong. As a parallel, think about banks. Most banks have rules making vacation time mandatory, as a direct target on internal

fraud – if someone can't be out for a week, there may be a reason why. Similarly, if someone needs to vet and potentially adjust reporting before you see it you may not be getting all the facts.

3. **Everyone's involvement** – The people who are closest to managing a function will be in the best position to assess what data is relevant. The best case is that they already have most of the data you need, through their existing management process. Then you truly know that they're managing their part of the business even without your inspection.

4. **Undistorted information** – Strive to use primary information. If the source data doesn't get you to the information and insight you need, look for ways to generate the right information from the system or process.

5. **Straightforward measurement** – The KISS principle comes in again. If someone has to be an expert to explain the data, you're not done yet.

6. **Sense of urgency and perpetual improvement** – Last week's data next Wednesday isn't going to support timely decisions. Understand how the data comes together and link reporting cycles to reasonable availability of the data. If the team provides their stats by end of day Monday, a good reporting process should be able to get you the information by Wednesday.

Now's the time to be truly fact based, so you have the information you need to sustain your growth in the grown up years.

Process

Teenagers have figured out a lot of what they need to know, and they think they know what they need to do. They've got most of the rules down, and a well trained teenager pretty much follows the rules or they can successfully fake it. When they make exceptions, teenagers generally know they're doing it and it's a calculated risk.

The critical shift to get to adulthood is to get them to think things through end to end. Taking a bus to unknown parts, as described earlier, the kid understood how to manage taking the bus. He knew to check the routes, find the schedule and make sure he has the right fare. He knew how to be at the right bus stop at the right time and how to pay the fare. The part that he didn't quite do was thinking the trip through to the end—what it would take to be home by his curfew.

Looking at processes 'end to end' lets you identify the things in the early steps that can make the process more effective, make the effort cost less, or give you a better outcome.

Consider the process that takes you from customer quote through to cash in your bank account. Lots of companies have processes to make sure that bids are solid and have the right cost models and approvals. Then they have processes to make sure that actual sales and delivery have integrity and meet the customer expectations (including, perhaps, quality assurance). They have separate processes again to handle invoicing and collections.

In most instances, if you line up those three disparate processes and get the people who understand them together in a room, you can find ways to improve steps along the way that will improve the results overall. Ideally, taking an end to end view lets you take your list of existing process gaps or problems and find cost effective ways between 'quote' and 'cash' to address them.

Teenagers are also sometimes lazy, which makes them adept at the benefits of automation. How much can they make happen without actual effort on their part ? For example, they might ask for a bus pass that takes out the 'right fare' part of taking an unknown bus. Next birthday, they'll probably be suggesting an i-phone, so they don't need to check schedules ahead because the web is available real time. Now's also the time for your business to be thinking about effective automation.

> *"You can usually find a management solution to a technical problem. There is never a technical solution to a management problem."*
>
> —Colin Rous

Once you've figured out your critical end to end processes, use that as the basis on which to prioritize on automation. In most instances you should fix the process first – then look at automation. Some software can help you structure the process, or a change in software could demand some change in process, so if you are looking at making investments in both process and tools in a short time frame it's worth planning for both in parallel. Then you can be informed making the trade-offs on how much to invest in which effort.

Process is the place where you get comfortable that if you had to put your daughter on the bus for college tomorrow, she would thrive.

Making Change

Most of us would never go back to being a teenager. The challenges and frustrations that come from both the physical changes and the responsibility changes are major. Most teenagers, though, don't want to acknowledge the fundamental state of flux that they're in. My son Geoffrey seems constantly surprised by the fact that in photos from two years ago I am taller than him ! Perspective is all about where he is now. It's as if it's all a big surprise.

One of your biggest challenges with 'growing up' will be getting acknowledgement and acceptance of the need for change. In *Beware the Naked Man Who Offers You His Shirt*, Harvey MacKay draws the same conclusion. "Most managers don't manage change. It takes them by surprise. What we're actually managing is the conflict wrought by change." [50] People who either don't see the urgency, or just object in principle, will be a distraction. Perhaps they'll object passively, just deferring action, but they may also resist with outward efforts to deflect or destroy. At this stage in your development it will be critical to be specific about areas for change, and to do what's needed to drive the focus.

> "Diamonds are only lumps of coal that stuck to their job."
>
> —B. C. Forbes

In *How to Behave*, Severe emphasizes that parents don't fail with their teenagers "because they are inadequate, but because they are inconsistent. They procrastinate. They don't follow through. They say things they don't mean." [51] He's empatheic—it's the nature of raising teenagers. "We become annoyed repeating everything three times. We spend too much time arguing. We become drained from nagging."

Taking Severe's advice, you'll pick your battles—be selective but clear about the changes that you need to see happen. Set targets – align quotas – demand buy-in. Make sure that by the time the kid is ready to go off to college he'll know how to thrive independently.

Planning and Managing for Growth

When it comes to planning, what's working in your favor is that teenagers want to be treated as adults. The parenting role is about helping them through that – but not taking it over. Marano talks about encouraging kids to problem solve and take risks. Let your kids know that there is more than one right way. "Innovation comes from seeing things differently."[52] Innovation will be key to your business growth plans, so it's critical to enable it.

A critical skill for kids to develop is the need to think about their surroundings – in college residence, they have to think about their room mates – in a job they need to think about the people they work with. As with kids, by leveraging your employees' desire to be given independence, and by supporting your employees in creating their own paths, you have the impetus to move them to a more cross-business focus. You're in a position to have planning start to take an enterprise view.

> *"In the old economy, the challenge for management is to make product. Now the challenge is to make sense."*
>
> —John Seely Brown

In the book *The Adaptive Enterprise*, Haeckel talks about the "medium term growth crisis"[53]. He stresses the need to deliberately create enterprise level outlets for new ideas, with the paradox being that "the best managers are in charge of the operating units. Their focus is on their results in the near quarters. They are in 'make and sell mode.' New business ideas have no outlet." If you're not encouraging new ideas at an enterprise level, "the new growth gap gets bigger – potentially insurmountable."

Once your planning starts to be done at an enterprise level, that process needs to be tightly aligned with an effective budget process. Good budgets need to have four characteristics:

1. **Be attainable.** That doesn't mean you don't 'stretch' your team, but they do need to envision some way to get to the numbers you've committed – you can't plan toward a target you can't see.

2. **Be fact based.** This is where the rubber hits the road—ensuring that metrics are supportable. It's difficult to plan if you don't trust the target not to move.

3. **Clearly define productivity targets.** Are you after producing more widgets, or making cheaper widgets? Usually it's one or the other. If you think you want both, make sure that someone is planning for the investment and what's got to be different for that productivity to be achieved.

4. **Support your values.** What are you prepared to compromise on? Employee satisfaction? Delivery to the customer? Quality? For example, the cost of a project is a three legged stool; time, scope and resources. You can cut any one leg shorter, and the stool will stand. Many small businesses have a four legged stool – the fourth variable being quality. We all know what happens when a four legged stool has one short leg. Would you approve a project plan and budget if you knew that quality

was considered dispensable to meet the rest of the plan?

You are what you spend. As you grow, you need to put planning in the hands of your employees. The executive scrutiny comes in the assumptions and baselines behind the plans. They are as critical to your sustainable growth as the plans themselves.

Now's the time to build a values-based and sustainable planning process. Move aggressively toward the kind of participative programs that will keep the whole team committed and align the business investment at an enterprise level.

People Strategies

Most teenagers have days that they're helpful and considerate – and days that they're not. Unfortunately, there are too many variables involved to even begin to understand or predict when which might occur.

It may not be much different in your business. Grown up behavior would have all individuals recognizing their roles and taking consistent responsibility for their contribution to the working environment. You're probably not quite there.

McKinsey in the 90's talked about the 'next great performance challenge.'—Who are the right people? What is the right informal network? What is the right culture?—Those are the people strategy questions that can keep you from growing up. In *The Milkshake Moment*, Little suggests you ask yourself "will winners want to work here?" He emphasizes the need to create a culture, an environment and a reputation that offers what people want in work.[54]

> *"The most important thing in any relationship is not what you get, but what you give."*
>
> —Eleanor Roosevelt

Don't assume that either age or tenure indicates an individual's business maturity. Based on Severe's advice in *How to Behave So Your Children Will Too*, there are five things to encourage with teenagers:

1. **Trust.** Ask opinions and show that you value them.

2. **Reinforcement.** Recognize hard work.

3. **Feedback.** Point out strengths and improvements.

4. **Improvement.** Encourage them to learn from mistakes.

5. **Responsibility.** Show them where they can decide, and then support them.[55]

Your teenager will tell you (with great disdain) that they don't want a hug – especially in front of their friends. The reality is that most do – in fact they need it. A successful parent picks their moments to dive on in anyway, and in the right setting they're tolerated. With all the other things pulling and tugging at the teenage brain, encouragement is critical to keep a kid grounded in the values that you've worked to instill.

Your teenage business has as many conflicting puts and takes – and can be as frustrating. As you invest in the right people to take you to the next level of growth, use genuine and regular encouragement to reinforce the right value systems and policies.

Little's book talks about having policy systems that support the environment and culture you want to create. His premise is that "stupid systems, pointless policies and muddled management" get in the way of real growth. He emphasizes people strategies and policies cause an organization to get in its own way. To break the cycle, you need the right policy system, and "it must be consistently reviewed and reinforced, be representative, and be regularly communicated."[56]

To move from adolescence to adulthood, you need to be able to identify and turn to the right people, and you need those people to be committed. Your people strategies are key.

Communication

Teenage communications are, in a word, limited. Communicating with an adolescent takes patience, resilience and a good sense of humor. They're easily offended if they don't feel you're taking them seriously enough, and they're quick to point out when you miss the point or don't know the lingo. When I'm talking with my kids, I spend a lot of time biting the inside of my cheeks to keep from laughing out loud.

Covey in his book *The 7 Habits of Highly Effective People* talks about communications in the context of "personal currency in the emotional bank account."[57] He stresses that "when the trust account is high, communication is easy, instant, and effective." Your focus now needs to be to build your personal currency with your people.

> *"The most important thing in communication is hearing what isn't being said."*
>
> —Peter Drucker

Covey talks about six major deposits to be constantly making to the emotional bank account[58] :

1. Understand the individual.

2. Attend to the little things.

3. Keep commitments.

4. Clarify expectations.

5. Show personal integrity.

6. Apologize sincerely when you need to make a withdrawal.

Your business, at this point, is on the brink of adulthood. You're the one who's going to get your employees to communicate like adults. What's said, and how it's said, is critical for you and for your senior management team.

Decision Making

Teenagers live in their own world. They know people there. They talk among themselves, but they seldom consult on decisions with the outside world. They don't mean to be arrogant—but in their self-contained way—they are.

In *The Accidental CEO*, Novak talks about his own experience at Pepsi. He was responsible for the launch of a product called Crystal Pepsi. Crashed and burned. It even became the subject of a parody on Saturday Night Live. Don Kendall, the founder of Pepsi Co, actually said "I don't like it, but if you do…" so off Novak went and launched the product. Novak attributes the whole debacle to "arrogance induced deafness." He had made up his mind, so he wasn't listening.[59]

The opportunity to take your team to a more adult level comes in getting them to genuinely work with you, and to consistently work together, using the 'know what you know and know what you don't' approach. Then you can ensure that everyone's ideas and knowledge are out on the table, and all things are considered before a decision is made.

> "A problem well stated is a problem half solved."
>
> —Charles F. Kettering

In his book *The Milkshake Moment*, Little stresses that "it's the people who have the courage to speak out who foster growth."[60] Encourage behavior that takes all input. It's not a sports competition—the only winner or loser is the business. There is only victory—when you get consistent focus on working together.

Leadership

Successful educators will tell you that the most important leadership attribute working with teenagers is authenticity. They are old enough, and most are smart enough, to know if you are genuine. They build up their adult behavior 'rules' from watching everything you do and don't do. Parents of teenagers spend a lot of time thinking and re-thinking whether they handled a situation as best they could – playing back conversations – debating going back to try to improve the outcome. It's a challenging role to play.

How to live up to that standard? Severe, in *How To Behave So Your Children Will Too*, talks about three critical 'promises'[61]:

1. Promise to have the courage to be open and accept new ideas,

2. Promise to have patience, and

3. Promise to practice.

Kids are going to become adults, no matter what we do. The big difference is whether the teenager gets on the bus to college feeling confident, and able to succeed. Whether you're the boss or not, if your company is striving to get through adolescence, it needs your leadership strength. As with the parent of a teenager, the spotlight is on you.

> *"If you do not tell the truth about yourself, you can not tell it about other people."*
>
> —Virginia Woolf

In the book *Working With Emotional Intelligence*, Goleman emphasizes the need for "emotional awareness" as a competence.[62] He suggests that an effective leader needs to:

- Know which emotions people are feeling and why
- Realize the link between those feelings and what they think, do and say
- Recognize how feelings affect performance
- Have a guiding awareness of their values and goals

With teenagers, the role models that they've embraced are what makes the biggest difference when they arrive at college and have to get off the bus and stand on their own. Think of leadership as that role model for your growing business. It can overcome gaps in other areas, and it can provide the inspiration to succeed. Moving to a sustainable growth model – a grown up business approach – demands leadership.

We consciously focus on getting the kid to get on the bus to college—'launching the child.' Think of that launching as the parallel to launching your business. You're moving from startup to steady state operations. The teenage years are when the parent – the boss—becomes the counselor.

Your biggest counseling challenge is to harness the creative power, yet to make sure that they're safe when they go off alone. In the book ***Empowering Innovative People***, Gretz and Drozdeck define four types of behavior, isolating that counselor behavior – 'executive behavior'—as what's needed to most able to effectively lead creative people.[63]

LEADER

Dictator	*Executive*
Bureaucrat	*Socialite*

HOSTILE   **FRIENDLY**

FOLLOWER

They define each of the quadrants as follows:

Dictator	- bully, dogmatic, control oriented – "I, me, mine" oriented - threats of firing a constant tactic
Bureaucrat	- prestige and power focus - rarely confront; shoot down with why nots and undermines
Socialite	- harmonious; rarely takes initiative
Executive	- independent thinking but respectful - makes decisions; sets limits

It's not difficult to imagine that the 'Executive' attributes would work best with a teenager. If you can prevent quick and adverse reactions to decisions or requirements, you can keep the focus and energy on the journey forward. Leverage the same level of "emotional awareness" to encourage and empower creativity and growth as you launch your business into the grown up world.

Driving the Autobaun

The Independent Adult

There's no one set of behaviors we can attribute to adults – just an underlying theme. If your business has made it to 'grown up' behavior, you're ready to pick the places that you really want to drive for growth.

'Grown up' is not a destination – it's a journey. If you're lucky, you'll keep discovering new turns in the road and around every turn there'll be new opportunities.

> *"The great French Marshall Lyautey once asked his gardener to plant a tree. The gardener objected that the tree was slow growing and would not reach maturity for 100 years. The Marshall replied 'In that case there's no time to lose. Plant it this afternoon.'"*
>
> —John F. Kennedy

You've reached the 'independent adult' column on the Maturity Profile. Now it's time to hone in on the things that are going to make a difference for your business. It's time to seek and find the differentiator in your industry. You're ready to drive to the real leverage that you need for growth.

The most value that this book can add at this stage is to take each of the business dimensions and describe how to find those last blasts of fuel that take you over the finish line.

This chapter brings together those final maturing thoughts that can put you into high gear for rapid and sustainable growth – a quick study version of some of the best practices and strategic approaches that really address the high growth challenge.

Contracts, Metrics and Process

You've aligned your ownership of process with the contract and metrics programs, to leverage the investments you make and to make sure that you realize the full benefit of improvements. You look for continuous and proactive improvement. You're confident that your business is being fact based, and your reporting is predictable and consistent. Most of the opportunity to make a process or measurement difference now is in your systems and technology.

In *Thriving on Chaos*, Peters talks about the need to "redefine the traditional process of measurement and control."[64] He emphasizes the importance of measuring " the right stuff" and sharing information. "Systems must abet our revolutionary agenda rather than impede it."

> *"The awareness of ambiguity of one's highest achievements (as well as one's deepest failures) is a definite symptom of maturity."*
>
> —Paul Tillich

Systems R&D may be as important for you now as product R&D. Your systems may not be what you need to handle the next exponential growth curve. Invest to fix what's not working, but if it ain't broke don't fix it. Invest, instead, in the 'realm of the possible,' so that when that next great revolutionary opportunity appears you're ready to take it.

Making Change

As a mature company, your business is running on all cylinders. Everyone's open and receptive to new ideas and opportunities for improvement. You're ready to put the pedal to the metal and drive for growth. Now you're ready to deliberately foster innovation and creativity.

In *Thriving for Chaos*, Peters talks about the need to be "a lover of change—a preacher of vision, shared values and strategy." He emphasizes the need for ideas to develop that are radical and 'bottoms up.'[65] Your 'growing up' foundation work has given you the tools to take that step. Have the courage of your convictions – drive for creativity.

> *"One doesn't discover new lands without consenting to lose sight of the shore for a very long time."*
>
> —Andre Gide

In their book *Empowering Innovative People*, Gretz and Drozdeck identify five key attributes of creativity:[66]

1. Being non-judgmental versus prone to evaluate quickly

2. Being reality based. Solve problems, don't avoid them. See problems as a challenge not a threat. Be spontaneous and independent.

3. Understand your beliefs and values. Rigid beliefs can affect the nature of your problem solving techniques.

4. Encourage divergent thinking. Actively explore different scenarios. Avoid convergent thinking which leads to a single right answer.

5. Consider the consequences. Look at all of the impacts to reduce the risk of being judgmental.

None of those attributes comes easily for most – we may be grown up, but we're still human. They all take commitment and focus. Trust in the foundation of your teenage years, and build on it.

Depending on your industry and growth strategies, innovation and making change may take significant commitment. Your entire leadership group needs to be working together, so take the time to make sure that you have agreement on what you want to be different. Then you can make sure that you'll empower the right changes and leverage the investments you've made.

Business commitment to change is critical. In *The Secrets of Discipline*, Morrish emphasizes that "faced with intimidating behavior, even adults become passive."[67] You can't afford to have ideas or input stifled. If you want speed, you need the car to be finely tuned and ready to engage.

Planning and Managing for Growth

Now you're faced with the real business paradox – the 'big opportunity trap' as Haeckel calls it in *The Adaptive Enterprise*.[68] Being grown up, you don't want to go and play with the kids when they come to call. Unfortunately, the kid that you ignore—the 'small' business idea that you reject based on an assumption of the size—may be the 'bridge' to the next great opportunity in your unfolding marketplace.

> *"Imagination is more important than knowledge."*
>
> —Albert Einstein

In *Who Says Elephants Can't Dance*, Lou Gerstner talks about "making the big bets."[69] The new opportunity was clearly going to be the integration of the pieces parts. Lou believed that products would commoditize and IBM's customers would value solutions as much if not more than the products themselves. Historically, IBM's solutions team was a group of technical folks of all skill levels, and services were a give-away with the purchase of boxes and wires. Imagine the reaction to the notion that the least valued component of the product food chain was suddenly the value-add differentiator.

Planning for the next exponential growth opportunity may demand that you look outside of what you do today, and outside of your business comfort zone. The foundational work that you did in the teenage years gives you the consistent and trusted operating practices you need. It's time for the team to manage the steady state business so you can be looking outward.

People Strategies

Now that you're an adult, you've got a steady date and a solid social crowd. You'll add new friends who'll fit your lifestyle and interests, and you'll plan activities based on what your friends like to do.

Your business has gone through the same change. Now it may be less about attracting new talent – unless you develop a new interest—you have the top talent you need. It's time to really focus on encouraging the talented people you have, and getting the most out of them.

People strategies are not just a high tech challenge. In *Winning Through Innovation*, Tushman and O'Reilly cite retailer Nordstrom as an innovator in motivating service oriented professionals to focus on their key differentiator – customer service.[70] All new employees at Nordstrom get a welcome package:

WELCOME TO NORDSTROM.

We're glad to have you with our company.

Our number one goal is to provide outstanding customer service.

Set your personal and professional goals high.
We have confidence in your ability to achieve them.

Nordstrom Rules:

Rule # 1: Use your good judgment in all situations.
There will be no additional rules.

Please feel free to ask your department manager,
store manager or divisional general manager
any question, any time.

Clearly Nordstrom decided that their strategic differentiation comes from their people. If every person you have contact with at Nordstom feels empowered to use their judgment, that trust will create support throughout the store to give you, the customer, the best possible experience. Nordstom delivers the power of the store one person at a time, with trust as the link that binds all of the employees together.

> *"Help thy brother's boat across, and lo thine own has reached the shore."*
>
> —Hindu Proverb

For a mature and empowered business, the power to grow is in the linkage between the people. In *The Adaptive Enterprise*, Haeckel talks about 'organizational clarity' as a key to the "coordinated strategic behavior."[71] He says that the challenge is to empower individuals and groups to make their own decisions, so that they recognize the need or opportunity for change and they are able to respond quickly.

As a grown up enterprise, empowerment shouldn't be a difficult decision – the challenge is in deciding what level of organizational coherence you need, and choosing a framework you trust to enable that.

Communication

As a grown up, you've pretty much taken control of the formal and informal channels. You're deliberate in what's said—how it's said—and who's saying it. Now is the time to formalize how you apply those learnings to the outside world. How do you communicate with customers and shareholders?

In *The Milkshake Moment*, Little emphasizes the importance of knowing that you did 'the right thing'—not just as "an ethical imperative, but as the clearest path to growth."[72]

If you know that you've done the right thing, you will have the conviction to say the right thing – you just have to decide who should say it and how.

Customers, on average, are looking for a 'satisfying' answer. That's not to say that you have to give them what they want, but it's an important grown up talent to manage their perception of what they get. If you ask 'was that a satisfying answer,' you can redirect the focus from whether the answer was the one that they wanted to whether the answer had integrity and told them what they needed to know.

One of the challenges of being an adult is also knowing what not to say. Once you have other investors or shareholders, you owe them a different kind of integrity. You're old enough now to watch Saturday Night Live, so it's time to learn about the 'cone of silence.' It's no longer appropriate to talk broadly about everything that's going on. As interesting as your acquisition plans may be at the Sunday BBQ or in the hall with employees, your Board of Directors has a right to assume that the company's strategies are contained until such time as they've made a decision.

> *"The best thing about not saying anything is that it can't be repeated."*
>
> —Susan L. Wiener

The cone of silence is critical to let your business run without distraction in times of change. It's human nature to think about the impact of changes on oneself. It takes a strong ethical standard for people not to try to influence things, if they can, to their best advantage. Talking broadly about things that aren't certain can alter behaviors and may end up adversely affecting the business or reducing the options that you can decide between. As a grown up company you need to have a new standard of care for what you communicate and how.

In a larger company, the decision makers on significant changes are often far removed from the front line people and the customers. Often the most significant impact of decisions and changes will have less to do with the decision itself and more to do with how it's communicated and what's said. As a grown up company, your communication strategies may become a critical factor in your success.

Decision Making

As grown ups, we've learned to anticipate problems or recognize them early, and then to ask questions – and listen to the answers – as the foundation for effective decision making. Your business decision making needs to be positioned for that same discipline.

In his book *Leading With Questions: How Leaders Find the Right Solution by Knowing What to Ask*, Michael Maquardt points to asking questions as the ultimate leadership tool. He sees questions as the foundation for effective decision making.[73] Maquardt draws credence to his views by pointing to some of Peter Drucker's definitions of the effective executive:

- They ask "what needs to be done?"
- They ask "what is right?"
- They listen first and speak last.

> *"It is better to ask some of the questions than to know all of the answers."*
>
> —*James Thurber*

In *The Adaptive Enterprise*, Haeckel recommends learning from Arthur Sloan at GM – "build context" for decision making by defining governing principles or ground rules that set the boundaries for acceptable behavior.[74] Not unlike speed limits on the highway, decision making ground rules can help reduce ambiguity, provide purpose, and clarify relationships in terms of 'who owes what to whom.'

Leadership

If you're going 300 mph in the race of your life, you can't be worried about whether your tire pressure is right. You have to trust the pit crew to have done their job.

If you're on track to realize your growth objectives, moving into high gear as a business is going to be the race of your life.

> *"We learn more from our errors than from our virtues."*
>
> —Henry Wadsworth Longfellow

When I was at IBM, one of the most meaningful investments that they made in me was a leadership assessment called 'Pathfinder.' The entire premise of the Pathfinder assessment was to refine my development objectives by identifying the leadership competencies where I excelled and taking those specific capabilities to a differentiating level.

As a grown up, you're soon going to be a little long in the tooth to start changing who you are and how you work. Be ruthlessly honest with yourself about what you do well, and what you don't. Accept that you enjoy some things more than others. Drive to differentiate yourself through the things you're good at. Trust in other peoples' talents to support your business on the things that you aren't.

CHAPTER FOURTEEN

Everything I Need to Know I Learned at IBM

Arguably Middle Aged

Many of us who are fifty or older are content with where we are. We're not done yet, but we're not trying to solve world hunger either. For the companies in that frame of mind, the focus is on mature governance. If you have stayed relevant to the market, you have the luxury of looking forward to a long and enjoyable middle age.

The successful middle age strategy involves being proactive to not lose touch with the market or your people—focused on improvement and developing the next generation of talent. You've paid the proverbial mortgage off, and your equity is now solid – what to do next ?

Some middle aged businesses, though, will have lost their relevance. Then they have to either retire or take more drastic mid life measures.

There is no better example of a mid life crisis than the IBM Lou Gerstner took over in the 1990's. He decided that he would settle for nothing less than the sports car on the Autobahn, so he had to figure out how to reinvent the business to bring back the passion for speed and agility.

Middle aged companies fail by looking backwards or sideways.

In 1979, IBM would have defined its competition as Amdahl, Fujitsu and all the rest. As a result, it virtually missed the microprocessor revolution and nearly tanked the company. Conversely, Gates didn't invent Windows, the spreadsheet, the GUI, or even DOS. He bought DOS from a bankrupt company, took his cues from Lotus and WordPerfect, looked at the Apple GUI, and..VOILA! Windows.

Apple didn't invent the GUI either...It was a guy called Alan Kay at Xerox PARC. Xerox brought the greatest interface ever to market, but insisted it be closed only to run Xerox software—you had to use their own spreadsheets. Killed the product.

Jobs at Apple saw it, copied it, and the Mac was born. Xerox and IBM had the wrong lens. Microsoft and Apple had the right one.

Yet Microsoft became middle aged. They completely missed the Internet, and only recovered late by bundling Internet Explorer with Windows. Fast recovery, but never total. And they never saw Google coming.

Through the Looking Glass – What's Different

It's just like Alice in Wonderland. You've watched this point on the horizon for a long time, and now it's in front of you. Looking into the mirror, everything feels the same, but it's not. They talk different, and they act weird !

They talk different

When I first joined IBM, I had been working for more than 15 years but I had never really observed at close range the way the long term IBM'ers talk. My first big project was with a wonderful woman named Jennifer. To this day, I remember just watching her mouth—trying to figure out how she could so easily find all and just the right words to be so clipped and succinct. I made a mental note to learn how to talk like her.

A few years later, when I was the CIO for the 10,000 person IBM Global Services business, I had a town hall meeting of relatively young managers and employees. At the reception afterward, one of the managers came up to me and said "I just love listening to you. I can't imagine how you so easily find all and just the right words to be so clear and precise."

They act Weird

Part of the reason that large companies work differently is the natural conflict that exists between the people who want things to stay the same and those who want things to be different. The way Lou Platt, CEO of Hewlett-Packard puts it, "We have to be willing to cannibalize what we're doing today in order to ensure our leadership in the future."[75] He emphasizes that at this stage in its growth, a company is "operating part of the time in a world of relative stability and incremental change and part of the time in a world of revolutionary change."

To manage that organizational schizophrenia presents a different set of challenges for your management team. On the one hand, you'll have people in your business who are enjoying the proverbial cottage and golf lifestyle presented by a stable customer and product base. They've reconciled themselves to their wrinkles and laugh lines. On the other hand you'll have people who look back at your history of growth and success, and they want the chance to get a piece of that growth for themselves. The steady state groups – those on the receiving end of the cannibalization – are going to be naturally fearful of the more aggressive folks trying to take the business back to the organizational equivalent of the 30 year old.

In *Who Say's Elephants Can't Dance*, Lou expressed surprise at the mere existence of a behavior he called 'push back.'[76] As an IBM'er at the time, I can attest – push back was alive and well as part of the jargon. Lou was amazed—he'd never heard it in any other company. He even saw examples of people fighting changes that had been made years earlier.

> *"To find fault is easy. To do better may be difficult."*
>
> —Plutarch

Your challenge in these more mature corporate years is to find the right balance. Once you determine what the balance should be, you can bring the whole team together to support both the base business and the innovation areas. This may be the biggest leadership challenge you'll face.

What to Do With Your Money When the Mortgage Is Paid?

A mature, arguably middle aged business has fewer levers to pull – less opportunities to differentiate. Even if you're not looking for your long lost youth, you need to stay relevant and avoid complacency.

To that end, there are two key areas for focus – leadership and your customer.

Leadership—What's your next generation?

Now's your opportunity to take leadership to a whole new level. Take, for example, the move to 'matrix' management as a necessity to support global management of large businesses. In the time leading up to the early 90's, large companies may have been operating Globally, but most maintained a fully accountable 'country level' General Manager. That was consistent with the business school teaching and general management doctrines that said you should provide employees with clear responsibilities and a single reporting line.

As true Globalization started to be both technically viable and operationally opportunistic, the notion of 'matrixed management' started to come into play. There might be local or country level people working in a specific area, but in addition to taking direction and being accountable to the local executive most employees also had performance measurements that made them line up with objectives to support the global entity. Working effectively in a matrix, where your objectives and performance measurements are actually held and governed by more than one person, is a very different working challenge – there needs to be a high degree of trust.

Matrix management was a good example of a place for push back in IBM. Lou specifically communicated his expectations of all IBM'ers as a general call to action for all employees. "Leaders have another critical attribute," he said. "They trust their colleagues. They say 'you've got the ball this time. What can I do to help?'"[77] Prior to Lou's email coming out to all employees on September 28, 1998, everyone wanted to either own a task completely, or have no responsibility or involvement with it whatsoever. Clearly Lou was close to what was really happening in the field—he took a strong leadership position by addressing the issue directly in an email to all employees. The push back stopped almost immediately.

> *"A moment's insight is sometimes worth a lifetime of experience."*
>
> —Oliver Wendell Holmes Sr.

Many mature companies also entrench their Business values in a set of defined 'competencies' – that becomes the focus for management development investment. For many companies, their focus on leadership is considered a key and strategic differentiator so competency programs aren't made public. Since Lou's published it in his book, it isn't confidential so we can use it as an example:[78]

Focus to Win	- Customer Insight
	- Breakthrough Thinking
	- Drive to Achieve
Mobilize to Execute	- Team Leadership
	- Straight Talk
	- Teamwork
	- Decisiveness
Sustain Momentum	- Building Organizational Capability
	- Coaching
	- Personal Dedication
The Core	- Passion for the Business

IBM invested both research dollars and soul searching to develop the list that they felt met their strategic objectives. They also put huge resources into assessing the leadership group to identify strengths and weaknesses. Their ongoing people strategies are directed at providing training and development – even significant developmental job assignments – to help build the right areas of strength. IBM specifically looked at key leadership teams to ensure that the combined strengths of the members reflect a balance and bring differentiating talents together for strength in the team as a whole.

Your Customer – What's different about selling to a big company, and how does that change what you do?

Most people who work for a large company today have had their jobs loaded up through iterative rounds of cost take out. Bureaucratic as they may seem, you can bet that for the most part they're not doing anything that they don't have to do.

Large companies are rigorous in their metrics, and performance evaluations, as a necessity driven by size. Individual and team compensation is usually tied very closely to those measurements. As a vendor to a large company, many things that your client asks for and does may seem curious – even counter-intuitive. If you're being asked to do something, or report on something, you can assume that the request is directly linked to some specific business metric someone is being measured on.

> *"The good thing about working with an IBMer is that they're maniacally focused on what they're being measured on. The bad thing about working with an IBMer is that they're maniacally focused on what they're being measured on."*
>
> —Rob Steele

In *Getting to Yes*, Fisher, Ury and Patton talk about "negotiation jujitsu." Their advice is to "assume every position is a genuine concern." By asking your client how they think different options would address the issue, you'll better understand the metrics behind the problem and you can help find your contribution to effective solutions.[79]

Understanding what your client is being measured on can give you significant insight into their business needs. At minimum it will make you more sympathetic. It may also have the benefit of making you more empathetic—helping you to anticipate or respond to their business problems.

Be Careful What You Ask For – You Just Might Get It

The holy grail for many entrepreneurs is to build something to a point and then capitalize on their efforts by going public. Unfortunately, many businesses decide to leverage a major event and do an IPO, and suddenly they find themselves with an interested and smart group of people called their Board of Directors.

> *"Funny thing – they do all that work to find really smart people to sit on their Board, and the next thing they know they've got a smart and interested group with the right to ask tough questions and expect answers."*
>
> —Jim Beatty

For the CEO and senior management team, what's really the difference between private and public equity?

In *What They Still Don't Teach You At The Harvard Business School,* McCormack describes it as follows:

"Profits, in and of themselves, are only important on Wall Street. In private companies, profits are practically irrelevant because all you do with excess profits is share them with the Government."

He goes on to talk about his own experience growing up—running a private company.

"In Phase 1 – the start up – all you think about is income. Do I have enough money to pay my overhead and keep things going?

"In Phase 2, despite your success at generating cash, you're not making profits. You become a little more disciplined about cutting costs, and the focus is on making your income more productive.

"In Phase 3, you finally realize that a private company is neither income nor cost cutting, but a carefully calculated combination of the two. That's when you start managing cash, making capital investments, increasing your asset base, or, as Ted Turner says, building value."[80]

As with going to work for a very large company, moving your personal equity into a publically traded company on an acquisition, or creating a publicly traded company yourself, demands that you go in with your eyes wide open.

There are shelves of books to tell you what you don't know, but be sure to understand the vagaries of Sarbanes Oxley (thank you Enron), a significant profit (Wall Street) focus, deep decision scrutiny, and less (potentially no) control depending on the Board of Directors. Understand how widely the shares are held and the market context for the valuation of stock. Where the bulk of the equity is controlled by one individual or group, understand their personal motivation and plans for the business.

It's easy to look at examples of the descent into middle age and wonder how such senior and experienced people can suddenly be so wrong. We don't suddenly become stupid. It happens slowly over time. As you go through the mature business years, if you're not focused outward, you're not focused.

> *"I didn't see it then, but it turned out that getting fired from Apple was the best thing that could have ever happened to me. The heaviness of being successful was replaced by the lightness of being a beginner again, less sure about everything. It freed me to enter one of the most creative periods of my life."*
>
> —Steve Jobs

Unless you want these to be your declining years, rekindling your business' creativity is essential to survival. For the true visionary, it's both what he sees and what he doesn't see that counts. You need to see the long term view, and ignore the obstacles.

Chapter Fifteen

The Cheat Sheet for the Final Exam

In Conclusion

To support rapid growth, a business needs sustainable and disciplined operations. There's no one right answer for how to achieve that, but there are answers that will help.

1. **Metrics and Contracts**

   - Measure what you know will drive success

   - Keep it Simple

   - Assess commitments to make sure that your planning models and your terms and conditions are aligned

2. **Process**

   - Build authoritative processes that are clear about what needs to be done and reported, by whom, and when

- Make sure that all processes drive to a necessary business outcome

- Enforce process compliance with logical consequences

- Take a participative approach to developing new processes

3. Making Change

- Be fact based; be neutral

- Don't shoot the messenger; encourage lessons learned

- Set the bar high; expect openness and integrity

4. Planning

- Encourage planning to be done by the people who can affect the results

- Take an integrated approach to consider all business factors and impacts

- Focus on what can be achieved

5. People Strategies

- Focus on recognition; understand what your employees value

- Recognize 'what' you do will deliver loyalty and commitment; 'how' you do it will demonstrate respect

- Encourage trust and respect throughout the team

- Take responsibility for the impact that you have

6. **Communication**

   - Use both informal and formal communication channels to the business interest

   - Plan how to communicate, to have the message heard

   - Plan what to communicate, to deliver the right message

   - Plan who should deliver the message to be most effective

7. **Decision Making**

   - Ask questions

   - Listen to the answers

   - Know what you know; know what you don't know

   - Take deliberate risks – Don't just let risks surprise you

8. **Leadership**

   - Be consistent

   - Say what you mean; Mean what you say

   - Expect accountability

   - Anticipate problems

   - Do the right thing

   - Be a role model

CHAPTER SIXTEEN

Know When to Stop Talking

Moving On

As this book goes to publishing, Geoffrey is preparing to make decisions and move on to the next stage – off on the bus to college.

Suddenly his teachers are marking differently. Things need to be not only done correctly, but presented correctly as well. English papers are marked on spelling, grammar and punctuation, even if that wasn't mentioned in the assignment. It's just assumed. Calculus answers have to correctly show all of the steps and logic – you can't skip steps, even if you are right.

It's driving him nuts!

But his teachers are right. Once he gets on the bus, he's arguably adult. He has to be ready to do it himself. And if 'do it' means taking a University level program, his work has to consistently be at that level.

His teacher in grade 8 did the same thing to prepare her students for grade 9. Until about February, it was brutal. But by spring break things were getting pretty easy. By May it was a breeze and the class was able to focus on the school trips and science fairs. Grade 9, which is very difficult for many, posed no significant challenge or adjustment at all.

He'll get through it. The toughest job for me, as the parent, is to stand behind the teachers and the process, and to support it as a necessary developmental step for him.

With work, as with kids, you won't always know if you're doing it right. You just do your best, and pick your times to stand your ground.

Be genuine and do what's right. You'll get it wrong sometimes, be ready to admit it.

As you conclude your reading of this book, think about how you measure your success. At minimum, be honest with yourself about that. Strive to let some part of your success be measured by the loyalty of your team and the respect that you've earned.

As Geoff prepares for the next set of challenges, it is actually Avery who has the biggest adjustment to make. Now she'll become the sole and only target for my little experiments in leadership!

> *"Go ahead and make mistakes. Make all you can. That's where you'll find success."*
>
> —Thomas J. Watson

Appendices

Learning from Others... Stories that Enlighten

When I was at IBM, one of the competencies that was identified as critical for all senior leaders was "breakthrough thinking." It was measured as a factor of common sense, intuition, innovation, street sense, experiential learning, theoretical reasoning and linguistics. You either had it or you didn't... there was no practical strategy for developing your competence.

I recently had the opportunity to read Roger Martin's book, *The Opposable Mind*[81] – finally a practical strategy to really hone these skills. I can't do it justice in these few pages, but it is based on the premise that discards the traditional thinking of "either/or" decision making. It provides practical strategies for developing your own ability to see the range of options and alternatives that exist "in the middle."

Martin's brilliance is in articulating the importance of recognizing your "stance"—the lens that you look through when you're dealing with a decision—in the context of the tools that you've collected and the experiences that you've had.

At any given time, you have a "stance"—you're looking through some specific lens that acts as a filter and places boundaries on your response. Martin shows you how to challenge your own stance and actively seek out other ways to look at the problem. He gives examples of activities he uses with MBA-level students, to help them leverage their different experiences and acquire different tools. He has successfully demonstrated that the more his students see and internalize their stance, the more they can see the shades of grey—they can proactively develop the range of options and alternatives that they have between two seemingly opposing choices.

If you want to develop your "integrative thinking," I can't recommend Martin's book enough. In the meantime, I've taken the lesson to heart and have added this section to *Growing Up*. Experience is critical to not gravitating to the "least bad" decision. These stories will bring to life some important experiences that I haven't had, but from which I have learned.

The stories in this section of the book are specifically chosen to broaden your stance—to offer a lesson that I haven't been able to offer from personal experience—to equip you with a few more tools, by way of examples, that you can draw on as you sort through the day-to-day complexity of your own business environment.

Jacoline Loewen,
Loewen and Partners

When the announcer yelled out, "The winner of the Media category, Ernst & Young Entrepreneur of the Year—Somerset Entertainment!" Andy Burgess grinned and bounded up to the stage to collect the award. It all looked so easy to be standing there in a tuxedo waving the trophy, but this moment of appreciation came from painful years of slogging late into the night.

Andy Burgess is one of the owners of Somerset Entertainment, which produces and distributes specialty music to gift stores and other non-traditional retailers using interactive displays where you can push a button and listen to the CDs. They have 28,000 displays in over 18,500 locations that now include mass merchants and specialty stores.

With business and Juno awards filling their shelves, Somerset Entertainment did various acquisitions and moved from $5M in revenues to $11M, until eventually they were achieving $21M in revenues. They bought a distributor and, in 1998, levered up with four flavours of debt: term debt, debt at 17% interest rate, revolving credit, and a vendor take back loan. Then the cracks began to show.

The Buffalo distribution fulfillment center had been shipping comfortably to over 100 different retail points when Andy asked, "Can you do higher volume?" Naturally, they answered, "Yes!" when in fact that was far from the truth. Somerset had been a company with $8M revenues and $2M in EBITDA (earnings before interest, tax, depreciation, and amortization—see glossary) but had grown into the supply chain approach with a distributor turning out to be slow and with the uncanny ability to mess up orders. They would say they had shipped goods—the display case with CDs—and Somerset would then invoice the retailer who, it turnrf out, had not received anything except a bill. It was October—prime pre-holiday selling time with the Christmas season around the corner. Not good!

American retailers are the toughest sons of guns and were furious at being bamboozled. They told Andy they did not get the goods, but then told him not to bother coming around any more—they were through. Yikes! In one fell swoop, Somerset had gone from being swift deliverers of orders to slow, unreliable duds.

"We hit $36M in sales with $8.5M EBITDA but our debt was at $15M and for the first time, we stressed about breaking covenants. We got a valuation of $15M and, with reluctance, we decided to go with a private equity investment of $21M."

In hindsight, Andy says getting private equity was good for the owners' motivation. It took the edge off the worry about money and retirement. "With private equity buying part ownership, we were allowed to take a large chunk out for ourselves straight away but still retain control. I had been working very hard and it was good to get $6M out for the founder and owners."

The money meant Somerset could pay off their debt straight away and still have $4M to make acquisitions. Andy says, "With that extra cash, we set up an office in Chicago that has turned out to be the vital springboard into the American market, taking Somerset to the next level. We've had a bad year in there, but we did not have to worry about the business blowing up. The peace of mind meant we could focus on battening down the hatches to the storm and finding a new way forward."

The private equity partners proved to be great sounding boards when Somerset was making acquisitions. The investors were more aggressive in wanting growth but respected Somerset's decision to step away from some identified targets.

"Also, when we nearly lost a key person," Andy adds, "The investors did bring him around and get him to stay."

Andy says, "When you are an entrepreneur working your butt off, it is great to get that cash pay out as well as have cash to grow the business. With private equity you get the best of both worlds—the cash liquidity without the rigorous scrutiny of the public market."

"Not every company can go public," says Andy. "Private equity will transition you." See if you can go public. Take Andy's test and put the necessary tick marks next to your chart:

✓ You are making enough money to pay for public listing and accounting.

✓ You are profitable.

✓ You have a strong growth curve for your revenues.

✓ You have a decent management team.

✓ You are a good size.

Andy says, "At the time of the private equity deal, we were too small to go public. With private equity investors, we got to retain control and we got liquidity. Private equity took us back from the brink with risky debt and looming covenants. They were the stepping stone to getting big enough until in 2005, Somerset did our initial public offering (IPO). Selling those secondary shares was sweet, too."

As Andy Burgess stood on the stage and let the applause of the audience sweep over him, it struck him how far Somerset Entertainment had come and what a ride it had been so far.

The number one issue for every entrepreneur is Money — getting money, raising money, convincing investors to give you money. Whether you are a start up, a family business, or a $100 million company, your biggest issue will always be money. Understand how different kinds of investment capital works, the benefits and pitfalls, how and where to find it, and how to be successful in attracting it. Put simply always take the money, but take it from smart people who can help you...

Jacoline Loewen is an experienced corporate consultant, lecturer and writer of business strategy. In recent years Jacoline has assisted owner-managed Canadian companies access capital, venture capital and private equity which requires a clearly defined five year strategy horizon. Jacoline shares her experience and business knowledge of Private Equity in her latest book *Money Magnet: How to Attract Investors to Your Business* published by John Wiley & Sons, 2008, which was selected as a textbook for The Richard Ivey School of Business.

When Director and Founder of Strategy International, Jacoline developed a strategic planning model and published it in a book called *The Power of Strategy* which went on to be a best seller. She also wrote *Business e-Volution*, which helped teams understand the business opportunities created by the Internet.

Jacoline works with client teams to address specific business issues, for example:

- New Strategies: Working in partnership with managers to develop new approaches to strategy. Helping teams shift to long term vision and know how to operate the growth strategies to achieve the goals.

- Measuring success: Establishing a few operating performance standards that will focus the organization and generate economic value.

- Revenue enhancement. Segmenting the market more effectively to accelerate market penetration, as well as generate more revenue from the existing clients.

- Branding. Defining brand positioning and assisting teams to live the brand through their work.

- Client Building. Designing approaches to deepen relationships with customers and increase revenue by developing both online and off-line communities.

- Cost savings. Identify and prioritize operational savings opportunities.

- Coaching. Helping senior management develop their leadership talent and giving executive feedback.

Currently a partner with Loewen & Partners Inc., Jacoline gets companies that want to grow "investor ready" and matches them with the best private equity partners. Loewen & Partners has raised $100 million for owners of companies. Jacoline also organizes CEO Roundtables and other conferences to transform the way CEOs and owners see their company and to encourage shared innovation and powerful growth.

Jacoline's other roles include serving as a judge for the UBC and the Richard Ivey School of Business' Business Plan Competitions, sitting on the University of Toronto's Rotman School of Management's MBA IMC volunteer board, mentoring for Canadian Youth Business Foundation as well as being a member of Canadian Association of Family Enterprises, Women in Capital Markets and The Ticker Club. She was on the Board of Directors of the Strategic Leadership Forum where she ran the Knowledge Café series. She is also a Board member for Bilingo China, Flint Business Acceleration, Innovation Exchange and The Women's Post. Jacoline organizes CEO Roundtables and hosts Financial Post Executive podcasts (available on iTunes) with The Richard Ivey School of Business as a co-host.

Jacoline holds an arts degree from McGill University and a MBA from the University of the Witwatersrand Business School. Her MBA thesis was published by Cambridge University, Jacoline was invited to present it at Cambridge's European Strategy & Operations Conference, and it was published by Cambridge's Engineering faculty.

Clients include government, not-for-profit, corporations and partnerships in North America and Southern Africa: Bermingham Construction, Spintex Manufacturing, Kids & Co, Innovation Exchange, CBC, Standard Bank, Nedcor Bank, Impala Platinum Mines, Liberty Life Insurance, Independent Newspapers, Vodacom, SABC, Eskom, Dept. of Trade & Strategy, Transnet, Telkom, Canadian Standards Association, etc.

John McKimm,
The Brainhunter Story

If you have growth ambitions, you will have to go looking for–and take–outside Capital. Be careful what you ask for… where that money comes from makes a huge difference to almost every facet of how you manage and operate from that day forward.

Brainhunter Canada Inc. is a leading provider of professional staffing services and solutions in Canada, with Global delivery capability. Supported by a proprietary recruitment platform, the Company has extensive preferred vendor relationships in both the public and private sectors. Through its established recruiting channels, the Company provides its clients with ready access to a deep talent pool, consisting primarily of IT and engineering professionals.

With approximately 220 employees and over 1,600 contractors on assignment, the Company offers contract and permanent staffing, payroll management, managed staffing, software, and recruitment solutions.

Following an IPO in 2002, Brainhunter has grown rapidly through numerous acquisitions and organically. Moving through 2009, the next stage for growth demands additional equity capital to strengthen the balance sheet and provide the financial flexibility required for sustainable and profitable growth, and to support key strategic market opportunities to accelerate that growth. The Executive and Board challenge that is not to be underestimated in *Growing Up* is how to best attract that Capital.

The Brainhunter experience taught me a lot about the difference in how you manage with private money as opposed to public money. I'll try to share those lessons.

Private Money

In the Private Capital domain, your primary measure of success is valuation against where you "need to be." *If you are meeting your budget and targets – doing a good job in the business of the company, as measured against plans – you are a success.*

Private Capital investors will often work closely with your business. They'll be actively interested, and the really good investors will looking for involved roles on an Advisory Board. These investors will look for a strong 3 - 5 year business plan, and they will measure your success against the objectives that are set out in that plan.

With Private Capital, you need to have a very strong budget process. You need to manage your performance against that budget closely and often - monthly, quarterly, and annually. Read Alizabeth's chapter on Planning at least twice !

With Private money, you will have control over your Board makeup, so look at all of the aspects of your business and populate your Board with people who truly have something to contribute – don't fall into the trap of filling your Board with old cronies and lawyers! Expect a lot of your Board, because they will demand a lot of you. Treat your Board as an asset.

Leveraging Private Capital, you will get visible investment from some strong business partners who can bring both related experience and common sense to the table. If you want to run a business where you have control over the levers that drive growth, focus on Private money.

Public Money

When you have publicly traded shares providing growth Capital, it dramatically changes the parameters of your business. You'll need to do three things: (1) Learn to love the term EBITDA (Earnings Before Interest, Taxes, Depreciation and Ammortization), (2) Learn to live quarter to quarter – your focus will be short term, and (3) Learn how to drive share price as the primary measure of success.

On my departure from Brainhunter in 2009, we had over $400 million in committed business backlog and a demonstrated value of the Talentflow Technology Platform in the $10 million license fee paid by Workopolis (and similar license agreements with other major clients). The valuation based on share price had the business worth $8 million. It makes no sense, but how do you fix it? *With public domain investors, you are measured by stock price, which is largely outside of your control. If your stock price is not meeting investor expectations, you are a failure.*

With public money (through an IPO), it's easy to believe that you are getting the currency you need for growth. Unfortunately, you're getting a few other things along with the currency. Public Capital dramatically changed the parameters of our business in a few ways:

- Regulatory requirements imposed significant additional operating costs, including Board costs, audits, reporting, listing fees and changes in the structure of our financing costs

- Regulated review and reporting requirements significantly reduced our latitude for management judgment, and became a dominating feature in both our management focus and our business calendar

- Cost reduction became a critical focus for improving EBITDA, ignoring the reality that growth does not come free; often the investments that needed to be made were refused because they would have a negative impact on EBITDA and carry no measurable short term value in the public domain

- Regulatory restrictions and Board directions significantly reduced our opportunity to provide the kind of genuine performance incentives we needed to achieve the desired growth targets

The lesson learned in taking on the world of public investors is to pay very close attention to the rules you'll live with – you are entering a world of very rigid Governance, so you won't get to fix it later. Get advice and help on all of the important areas, including balance of control (you/ shared / Board), management contracts (your role and remuneration); how you will handle partnership agreements and new ventures; operational expenses that will change due to the regulatory requirements (don't commit to objectives – publicly or internally – without making sure that a "new" operational model is clear); and performance incentives like options, for you and your senior growth team.

If you want to grow, you have to take outside money, and no matter how you do it investors are ruthless. The trick is to understand enough about HOW you plan to grow, and how you want to manage, before you decide what kind of money to look for. Then be smart in who you team up with, and how you structure those deals – *go in with both eyes wide open and be sure that you are fully informed! Do your homework !! If in doubt, hire smart help!!!*

If you think you want to IPO, look at it as "an end", as well as perhaps a beginning. Make sure that the IPO event, in and of itself, leaves enough money on the table for you to be satisfied with what you have – you've got to be able to take out a significant portion of your personal risk – the IPO event should to some significant degree deliver on your base financial target. If you can't make the IPO a viable exit point, or you decide to continue with the enterprise for other reasons, protect the base that you have and then go forward as a new venture. If the IPO is unlikely to make that kind of money happen for you, and you really want to see the business through to the next step – stick to private money.

 John McKimm is a senior bottom-line-focused executive with extensive experience in public markets, financial management, capital markets transactions, financial restructuring, merchant banking, mergers and acquisitions, business valuations, marketing financial and advisory services, developing and managing effective investment teams and strategies, and creating, evaluating and executing investment opportunities. His experience in research, corporate finance, capital markets and financial advisory projects has crossed numerous industry sectors including regulated industries, retailing, distribution, manufacturing, waste management, telecommunications, computer hardware, software, real estate, financial services, petrochemical, food processing and select resource sectors. Assignments and projects have required extensive dealings with chartered banks, accounting firms, private placement sources, venture capital investors, investment dealers and retail and institutional investors across North America and Europe. Financial restructuring and investment situations have involved substantial operating involvement, both day-to-day and strategic. Investment situations in the past decade have been primarily technology focused, with strong emphasis on strategic and financial turnarounds, emerging growth companies and acquisitions.

John has served on many Boards, including Altus Income Fund, Rice Capital Management Plus Inc, Xycorp Inc. Midas Capital Corporation, Casierra Diamond Corporation, High River Gold Mines Ltd., International Energy Services, Inc., Midland Walwyn Capital Inc., Richardson Greenshields of Canada Limited and Prudential-Bache Securities Canada Ltd. He has a Bachelor of Laws degree and an MBA from the University of Western Ontario.

Bryan Pearson,
The Loyalty Group

I've always thought about the growth of a business in four stages.

First there's the 'fly by the seat of your pants' entrepreneurial stage – building the business idea, getting investors, leveraging what we knew to get support for the plan. That maps pretty well to Alizabeth's raising the toddler discussion – constant attention required to keep the kid safe and make sure he won't fall down the stairs.

Stage two is where you start to 'professionalize' your processes and systems – scalability of financing, stability of IT platforms, and focus on customer service. The kind of focus and attention it takes maps pretty well to being the parent of a nine year old. You can't be beside them all the time, but they still need a lot of guidance, so you weigh off the risks... how likely things are to happen... what's the trade off on consequences. You put your money and attention on the things you're likely to need next.

In stage three, the teenage years, we shifted the focus to acquiring major accounts – Pharma Plus, American Express, LCBO. That shifted our focus to building maturity in how we attracted and managed accounts. The success of that effort gave us the footprint in the market to grow the business to the next level. Over a 10 year period, we grew revenue by a factor of 4 and EBITDA by a factor of 8. Customer activity in the form of redemptions took off. We were amazingly successful – so then we hit the limits on space, volume and IT capability. Fortunately, we had intuitively done what any good parent of a teenager does – we had set limits, provided a framework for growth, and closely aligned the growth strategy with our capabilities and priorities. Our teenage years were a time of galvanizing the vision and building a sustainable plan of attack.

We are now, arguably, adult, and we're able to loosen the boundaries and start to build some agility.

As a parent of teenagers myself, I get the importance of letting the kids make decisions – make mistakes. I've also seen how important it is to set boundaries – you have to provide context and parameters for making decisions, so that nobody does anything permanently disfiguring or life threatening.

Our approach to planning for growth is probably the best specific example of our response to the earlier challenges and demands of being a 'teenage' business. We had the benefit of a very strong 'mom and dad' team in our then CEO and CFO. They knew the importance of the financial controls and management process integrity, but they also knew that we needed to invest and innovate. Their response was a very disciplined and structured approach to planning for growth. We proactively applied Chris Zook's *Profit from the Core* model – investing in logical adjacencies and taking the investments in the right time and place to have the most appropriate impact. We also turned down some opportunities that didn't logically fit within the timelines and strategies that we'd set out with the parent company and Board. By looking at the logical next opportunities in context, rather than as specific targets for acquisition, we were able to do a really solid job of assessing all of the target opportunities to find the ones that would meet our growth objectives and add the most shareholder and client value.

As we got further into that discipline in planning, we also understood how important it was for everyone in the business to understand what we were doing – and what we weren't doing. In the summer of 2008, we actually published a book for internal use by all employees, clearly communicating "our path to a billion." That book talks about the top eight factors we're applying to achieve our targets for growth – the four "whats" and the four "hows."

Every employee at LoyaltyOne knew that we had committed to a four level plan for business growth – the four "whats:" core growth, collector revenue, new ventures and acquisitions. They also know the four "hows" – how we would ensure that we had the right people, culture, knowledge and processes in place to achieve our goal of becoming a billion dollar company by 2010 – engaged workforce, thought leadership, effective operations and product development.

Each member of the Executive Committee owned one of those dimensions. In spite of the challenges that any business faces, we've made superb progress. That success has moved us to a point where we can stop being directive.

Think of it as giving a teenager an allowance – there's an implied restriction on the allocation and use of those resources. We were doing the same thing. Alizabeth tells me that one of the unique attributes she found as our CIO was the relative absence of 'skunk works' – unauthorized projects didn't really exist here. In retrospect, I think that's true, but I don't know if it was the best thing for our growth. We had a strong technology innovation role in Alizabeth's team – they brought ideas to the Executive Committee – and if the idea was approved we found a way to sponsor it in the business for the next year. We potentially were limiting our ability to be agile – all of the energy went into getting approval or holding legitimacy for investment money rather than continually assessing new ideas in the broader business context of committed strategies.

The Grown Up Plan for Growth

As we move into a relative stage of adulthood, we're able to move to a more abstract approach – less directive and more of a "path to leadership." We're shifting our focus to a discussion of the *horizons of growth,* to make sure that we get to the revenue that we need over this three year period. This new stage in our development demands that we find ways to enable the right intuitive behavior for growth and innovation. We now specifically allocate an "innovation fund," recognizing that we're not going to know everything at budget time, and some things shouldn't wait until next year. As Alizabeth says, *we don't know what we don't know.*

As we progess on our three year path to a billion dollars, we've re-published the "top 8" book, refining the vision and emphasizing a context for growth rather than being directive – for the next few years we're focused on a couple major themes, with an underlying emphasis on the people – *Building an engaged workforce.*

Everything we're trying to achieve at LoyaltyOne depends on having a team of energetic, committed people who are proud of what we've accomplished so far and inspired to make this business even better as we pursue our future goals together. With these far-reaching goals in mind, we're focused on developing talent, promoting leadership, and fostering collaboration. We're recognizing our grown up capability to count on the people to take us to the next level – having a team of energetic and committed people who are inspired to make this business even better. It's all part of *Growing Up.*

Alizabeth tells me that her experience at LoyaltyOne was the inspiration for the Growing Up business model, and I understand that. She worked with us in the "teenage" years. As she says, "we'd built an amazing product, world class customer service, and strong core systems capabilities that would stand the test of time. We were one of those fortunate enterprises with threefold growth and no limit to our potential. Good as it was, our infrastructure was just not up to the size, complexity and business expectations for sustainable growth."

Our teenage years involved a lot of heavy lifting to move the Airmiles systems and processes to the kind of maturity and sustainability that we needed. Having intuitively taken a strong 'parental' role through our adolescence, we've emerged in a level of adulthood that positions us to meet the business expectations of a $1B run rate over the next 3 years – and the team is ready for the challenge.

As President and Chief Executive Officer of LoyaltyOne, Bryan Pearson leads all of the enterprises organized by Alliance Data under the LoyaltyOne umbrella: LoyaltyOne Canada, LoyaltyOne U.S., LoyaltyOne Consulting, the AIR MILES Reward Program, COLLOQUY, Direct Antidote and Precima. Joining the organization soon after its founding in 1992, he moved through a series of progressively senior roles, becoming President of the AIR MILES business in 1999 and assuming his current position in 2006.

Bryan is a highly regarded expert on enterprise loyalty, retail marketing, coalition marketing and customer relationship management. He is a frequent speaker at industry events around the globe, and his views are widely quoted in national and international publications. He also contributes to *COLLOQUY* magazine as a writer and a member of the editorial board.

A strong supporter of many community and charitable groups, Bryan is a board member of the Special Olympics Canada Foundation. He is also an active participant in the Venture Management program at Queen's University.

Judith Humphrey,
The Humphrey Group

As I read Growing Up, *I realized that the book's metaphor applies to my company, The Humphrey Group Inc., and shows the excitement of how we have grown the company.*

The Humphrey Group started out as a small, but sturdy toddler, dedicated to teaching executives how to communicate. Coming from a background in speechwriting, I saw the need for communications training at the executive level. The executives I had been writing for wanted to be inspirational, but they needed coaching in how to bring their scripts to life! There simply was no company that provided this service. Over lunch with a Los Angeles-based actor, Marshall Bell, we planned the firm: I would teach executives how to create their talks, and he would show them how to bring them to life. Our big idea was born!

Creating a new company was a daunting experience, and Marshall and I were happy to have the "parental" advice of a wise equity partner, Chet Posey. He had been Vice Chairman of McCann Erickson Worldwide. (Think of Bill Gates' decisions to hire Frank Gaudette as the first CFO.)

Chet was retired and was looking for an emerging business to nurture. He was a wise soul with much communications and marketing experience. He gave me valuable advice ("Put Humphrey in your company's name – J. Walter Thompson did it, and look what it did for him!") Chet helped me design our "brand" and develop our marketing material. Chet lived outside Canada, so he also introduced me to many US CEOs who would become our clients. Within a few years I was successful enough to buy him out, but he played an invaluable "parental" role in getting The Humphrey Group off the ground.

The transition from toddler to adolescent came as I expanded the company and brought in a group of Toronto-based actors as coaches. Marshall was still in Los Angeles and wanted to concentrate on his film career. So I brought in a team of local actors – from the stage, from TV, from director roles. Call it our "creative teenager years," a time when we took a look at ourselves and shaped a more individualistic corporate identity. The decision to bring in theater folk was one of the best choices I ever made. The actors were able to take clients beyond a narrow focus on business and technical concerns, and help them realize the importance of *how* their messages would be heard.

My coaches were young, creative types who brought enormous talent and presence. You wouldn't call me the "parent" but I was certainly a big sister. One of the actors, for example, had a presence that I felt executives could benefit from, but I knew he didn't have the money to dress for the business world. After I hired him, I took him shopping and bought him a Boss suit.

I also developed a methodology that I taught my coaches in a series of Master Classes. The lessons included rigorous instruction in listening, messaging, structure, language, delivery, PowerPoint, off-the-cuff speaking, and handling questions. We analyzed scripts of all kinds, openly critiquing them and honing our skills. I observed them teaching, and gave feedback. ("You can be stronger....you are dealing with executives who want your honesty and sound advice.") I learned from my talented coaches as much as they did from me.

Culturally I was creating an organization of people who were sensitive to the best interest of our clients. I taught these actors business acumen ("study each company... understand the issues"), how to dress ("lose your turtle neck") and how to relate to the client. These were our teen years... But adolescence passes for individuals, and it did for our company as well.

As a mature company, our intellectual capital has broadened. We added group seminars, which allowed executives who had our one-on-one coaching to bring this training to their teams. The outcome was some of the most successful communications programs in North America. We developed *Speaking as a Leader®* for men and women, and *Taking the Stage®* for women. This latter program, launched in partnership with IBM, has been a great success. Globally, it has reached over 50,000 women in IBM, Microsoft, Nortel Networks, TELUS, Dell, and Scotiabank. Michael Dell among others warmly endorsed it.

We are now much bigger – and my dealings with the world are more complex. I now spend more time with lawyers, support staff, and in training new individuals.

Perhaps the clearest sign that I had moved from "adolescence" to full maturity was the entry of my son, Bart Egnal, into the business. He has now been with The Humphrey Group almost a decade, learning the business. With Bart, The Humphrey Group has a strong and talented senior leader who will oversee the next stage of growth and diversification. He recently opened an office in Vancouver, B.C., to serve our clients in western Canada.

If I served as a "big sister" to my actors in our adolescent phase, today I feel I'm more of a "parent," especially to the young professionals who've joined our firm in the last few years. A recent example comes to mind. I decided to create a full-time consultant position to be filled by someone from outside our "troupe." With his business acumen and corporate experience, Rob Borg-Olivier fit the bill – and I certainly didn't have to buy him a suit, because he has a lot of polish! As is the case with most parents, I wasn't always the soft touch. But with the right guidance and mentorship, Rob has come into his own as a first-rate senior coach, and was recently appointed vice president. I am confident he will build on this foundation and achieve further success for The Humphrey Group in the years ahead.

I continue to "parent" the younger people in The Humphrey Group. We have a large group of 30-something professionals, all articulate, savvy, well-appointed and talented individuals who are learning how to build the business, teach, and administer. I am very proud of them all, and of the company.

Today we have a name, a brand, and a track record that mark us as a company that has "Grown Up" over the last 20 years – we are now the leader in our field. Our programs are known and used internationally. Our actors have travelled to Europe and Japan to deliver our courses. We work with a range of industries in many countries. Our women's program remains a global success. We are financially strong. Our revenues have steadily climbed.

What lies ahead? The young people in our company will continue building our name and reputation! We have an intergenerational culture, and one that will continue to serve our clients well. And I will, like a proud parent, look on and smile because we have Grown Up so successfully.

Judith Humphrey, President of The Humphrey Group Inc., is a pioneer and leader in the field of executive communications.

Raised in Connecticut, Ms. Humphrey earned B.A. and Master's degrees in English Literature at Indiana University, and completed Ph.D. course work at The University of Rochester. She came to Canada to teach at York University, where she was a humanities instructor for eight years.

Ms. Humphrey entered the corporate world and became a speech writer for a series of CEO's of multinational companies. In 1988 she established The Humphrey Group to support a still broader group of executive leaders. This Toronto-based firm teaches executives and senior managers how to create and deliver powerful messages in their speeches, presentations, informal remarks and everyday conversations. The overall goal of our coaching is to instill in our clients the ability to inspire and motivate others through all their communications. This approach combines high level leadership goals with the development of strong, strategic communications skills that advance those goals.

The Humphrey Group is comprised of highly trained professionals, many of whom have acting backgrounds. The firm is a leader in its field, and Ms. Humphrey has built an organization that is recognized in Canada and around the world for its ability to develop strong, influential leaders.

Ms. Humphrey has authored many articles, and her speeches have been reprinted frequently. She has built partnerships with The Niagara Institute, Southern Methodist University, and many corporations, including a global partnership with IBM. She is a member of the International Women's Forum, and has a husband and two sons.

Andrew Long,
Critical Pathfinders

Our business has been Global right from the outset, taking advantage of the incredible reach that the web makes possible. We had to specifically pick places to be 'Grown Up' right away or we could not be successful. Our product is a Process – *so we took the time to make it effective, and we always follow it. We have a large number of temporary employees, so* People Strategies *are also critical - we took an aggressive "buy" approach to get to maturity quickly.*

Critical Pathfinders is in the business of providing high value team building and team training programs in Canada, the USA and overseas. Over a ten year period, we have delivered over 1,000 successful programs to corporate groups in virtually every industry, ranging in size from under 10 to over 500 participants. Our vision is a world in which everyone loves their work, and we strive for excellence in program delivery and client satisfaction.

Process

Sustainable growth, for us, is absolutely dependent on ensuring that the program is delivered the same way every time. Our commitment to use local resources for program delivery whenever possible has demanded that we apply rigorous attention to developing effective process – and making it effective in practice. Critical elements of our process that are always applied include:

1.   A combination of training tools including conference calls, documentation of what to do and how to do it, scripted key materials like the session introduction, online video training, and conversation / rehearsal prior to each event by phone

2.   A detailed timeline for each event, including a final pre-event review call with the on site leader, regardless of the number of times that individual has run the workshop

3.   Post-meeting process including identification of all participants, gathering of feedback through an online survey, and a follow up call with the client for ways to improve, and the collection of testimonials and referrals

The advantage of having 'Grown Up' processes is that we can let the on site leader go ahead and manage the event independently. Despit our skill at planning for all contingencies, during the events there are sometimes decisions to be made by the leader without first seeking approval. They just tell us what they did afterward. I have a high degree of confidence and trust that our leaders can deliver successful events – and they do, every time.

People Strategies

Many of our session facilitators come to us through social networks – personal introductions, and even LinkedIn. We also have to accommodate the legal requirements and employment standards in all the countries in which our program is offered. It would be pretty easy to get in trouble. Clearly we don't have conventional people strategies for finding and evaluating staff – and we will probably never really invest in significantly 'Grown Up' programs because our full-time staff is so small.

To make sure that we develop and use really capable session facilitators, without over-investing, we take a sort of internship approach. The first time someone works on one of our events, they are in a helper role only. We then look to the event leader for feedback on how they did, and what it would take to develop them to more independence.

The most critical competencies we look for are that they respect the framework or process, and they think for themselves in delivering a quality event. If they help with an event and demonstrate those abilities, we will help them move forward on future events. Unfortunately, if they don't, they won't.

One of the toughest things about being so far removed from our "staff" is that we have to rely on the judgment of the people on-site and the feedback from the client. Many small companies have to contend with personalities and positioning. Our People Strategies spare us from that – we can just be fact based.

We had an event in Orlando. I got a call on my cell phone at 8pm the night before the event. The leader was coming in from Texas and the fog was so heavy her plane could not take off. Yikes!

The next morning at 8am we were on the phone to local Destination Management Companies. For our 11am event, we had to find a leader, brief her, get her the required documentation, teach her how to run the event and get her to the site. We got it done and the event was a success. Whew!

Without the process & the trust-based people strategies, we could never have saved this situation.

Andrew Long is the co-founder and president of Critical Pathfinders. Critical Pathfinders and its sister company Scavenger Hunt Anywhere provide team building, performance enhancement, team development and training to corporations in Canada, the USA and overseas.

Since 2000 he has worked with hundreds of groups and thousands of participants, creating and leading them through a wide number of powerful and engaging team building events, performance enhancement sessions and training sessions.

He consults in a diversity of areas including corporate strategy, workforce performance, team development, team building, employee attraction and retention, corporate training and internet marketing.

Prior to starting Critical Pathfinders, Andrew spent 3 years as a Financial Consultant for Merrill Lynch Canada and then 3 years in sales and marketing at Canadian Pacific Railway.

Andrew is an expert in team building, team performance and the skills and actions required for people in a corporate setting to work as effectively as possible together. Andrew is driven by his vision of a world where everyone loves their work.

Michael Della Fortuna,
Sal Oppenheim

Having spent the last 20 years or so working for both a variety of public and private companies, I have had the opportunity to experience de ja vu a number of times – it's often the same story over and over. The organizational chart looks like a family tree in my small clients – the corporate culture churns out a global army of clones to replicate its model in my large clients. In the end, companies differentiate and grow because they can turn a vision into reality – to execute an objective - to harness and leverage resources and be profitable.

This continual assessment is necessary to achieve one of the fundamental things Alizabeth discusses – sustainability – if the organization can not sustain itself it can't continue to grow, and it may cease to exist.

There are many 'rags to riches' private companies that have spent their time building a business without consideration to developing an organization. Businesses are built on markets and products - services and strategies. Organizations are built with individuals – focusing on a vision, common values and core objectives – a company spirit. Organization is the sustainable platform on which a growth oriented enterprise can be built.

The definition of sustainability changes during the life cycle of an organization. Initially it may mean maintaining cash flow to keep the doors open and lights on, it then changes to mean funding for the next product development or the acquisition of a new technology or another company. In many public companies the sustainability centers about share price and 'hitting the numbers' – the other sustainability factors follow from there.

Regardless of the which definition applies there is an event that impacts all companies equally, regardless of size, type, years of service; the event is the transition period from one leader to the next – the true measure of the sustainability of a company.

The Comparative Cases of CanWest and Rogers

Two very similar companies have recently approached the transition to a new leader – in the same time period, and in similar sectors – Rogers Communications and CanWest Media.

There are a number of similarities and differences between Rogers and CanWest – between Ted Rogers and Izzy Asper. One might observe that one leader built a business, the other built an organization.

Ted Rogers questioned the sustainability of his business and began to seek out a capable and willing management team of seasoned professionals. He looked for individuals that could understand his vision, grasp his intentions and foster the spirit of the organization. He knew he had to enable the organization to take root and become self sufficient. Rogers now has undeniable market strength and is in the capable hands of a management team that have the best chance of continuing to build a sustainable enterprise.

CanWest Media on the other hand was often referred to as being an "Izzy-run" company. In 1994 Mr. Asper said, "We're training the kids to be owners....they aren't being trained to run the place...they have the option to buy each other out if they disagree with how the business is being run."[82] Building a sustainable organization seemed not to be a priority, and with Izzy's passing the news suggests that CanWest is at serious risk.

Every leader has to build an organization. Sustainment has nothing to do with products, services or markets and everything to do with the development of the organization. The power in a company comes from the ability to leverage the founder's vision, replicate a model, and make consistent decisions based on a solid foundation. I have to believe that Ted Rogers surrounded himself with individuals – they understood and believed in his philosophy, and could direct the company with the spirit that Ted envisioned but without Ted in the room.

In the case of CanWest, it appears as if Leonard was not in lock-step with his father's philosophy. Izzy's more sudden death left the business with organizational gaps that Leonard must now figure out how to fix.

Creating sustainability comes with the building of an organization – not just building a business.

Sal Oppenheim

In 1789, Salomon Oppenheim opened a commissions and exchange house – converting currencies and extending credit. Today, Sal Oppenheim is the largest independent private banking group in Europe. This organization has endured for 200 years, and is a seventh generation family run company.

That's sustainability.

The entity was built on solid values and all those involved in the firm fostered the spirit of the organization. The growth and stability came not from products or services but from the ability to have key leaders make decisions that reflected the essence of what the organization was founded upon. These individuals were not only capable in their profession; they were able to nurture what was of value to the spirit of the company. This allowed the organization to change without having to compromise.

For Sal Oppenheim what is and has always been fundamental is being able to maintain values of independence and genuine self-reliance. The long-term preservation of values has been a fundamental goal enabling the growth of assets for future generations. In essence, Sal Oppenheim works toward the future rather than just the immediate outcome - virtually guaranteeing their sustainability.

It may seem easy when one has an entire organization focused on solid values providing focus and guidance. The challenge comes in maintaining these values while still meeting the needs of the market and remaining profitable – realizing continual growth. Though rich in tradition, they are a young and vibrant firm, and they have a variety of innovative offerings that provide future-oriented solutions for their clients.

In reviewing Sal Oppenheim it seems like an easy recipe – focus on core values, preserve capital, be future oriented – but it's difficult, extremely difficult. Take the ever popular asset backed paper, sub prime mortgage, derivative products that were all the rave until the last 12 months. Many large global organizations have fallen due to their exposure in these markets. Sal Oppenheim's reliance on their core values kept them away from these offerings, and they have not been impacted by any of the downfall that came with the collapse of the market. Think how difficult it must have been to avoid the temptation to enter a market where everyone was active and seeming to profit. In evaluating these opportunities Sal Oppenheim reviewed the offerings, the products, the services - they were not in line with the business objectives, so they did not engage. That's grown up planning for growth.

Building an organization is tough work, difficult decisions have to be made. Being private, the discomfort of many decisions becomes more apparent. Ensuring sustainability means doing what is best for the organization. The bigger an enterprise gets, the less 'family first' is the answer. An enterprise the size of CanWest or Rogers has thousands of committed an loyal employees depending on the leadership to consider their interests and livelihood – they're all counting on 'the parents' to keep the lights on – that's part of the legacy.

In Sal Oppenheim there are some 46 family members that have some controlling interest in the company. That said, it is not always a family member at the helm. Having the right person leading at the right time supports the sustainability of the organization; that's Sal Oppenheim's legacy ... "for future generations."

PowerSURE

PowerSURE is a client of mine with the wisdom to build in sustainability from the onset. Though countless hours are spent on markets and products (keeping the doors open and lights on), the same amount of time is being spent understanding how decisions today will impact the future.

Though it is definitely easier for anyone to run off and make a decision on their own, at this stage PowerSURE holds a lot of mini meetings, bouncing ideas off each other and ensuring that everyone is thinking the same way. In the PowerSURE office there is a crystal ball on one of the partner's desks, if you ask him if it works he respond by saying, "if we all sit around the table and see the same thing, that's as good as it gets."

The Three Practical Questions

After 20 years of working with both private and public companies, most of my client work is helping to address sustainability concerns. I'm working with a family business now that exemplifies Alizabeth's model. The founder is now building a transition plan that will formalize the organization, dispersing both responsibility and authority. My client is looking at both compensation and roles so that he can take on young and talented individuals – he's after the energy to drive the organization forward AND the patience to understand that 20 years of history can not be changed in a quarter or two.

Most 'young' businesses don't give attention to building a sustainable organization, and then they have to try to catch up – all of a sudden trying to go from being the energetic and eager youngster straight to the mature and responsible adult with a high degree of organizational maturity. Unfortunately, they have to start at the top and make sure that the right leadership is in place to bring 'the kids' along.

For the business owner looking at whether their legacy can be sustained, there are three simple questions to consider:

- Do the people leading the organization with you have the ability and desire to take on the challenge - do they understand the vision and can they foster the spirit of the organization into something executable by both them and their staff?

- Has your current management team demonstrated the ability to operationalize the vision or have they continually relied on your guidance?

- Can / will the current management structure work under a new leader?

Though these are tough topics to address, it is only the beginning. How will your 'baby' fare when you are no longer at the helm?

Early on in my career, I thought that founders and owners were staying on because that was all they knew — they worked so hard at building their company that they didn't know how to let go. The fact of the matter is that many can not let go because the business can't survive without them. So much of the company depends on them that if they walk away they will surely be the contributing factor to it's demise. They've realized, too late perhaps, the importance of making sure that while the business grows, they are truly Growing Up.

Michael Della Fortuna's background could not be more varied. A former Air Force Officer Michael has worked in some of the most stressful environments. Taking his ability to execute to the civilian world he has held leadership positions for a number of public organizations including Lear Corporation, General Electric, Husky Injection Molding and L-3 Communications – SPAR Aerospace. Having had the privilege to work for these global companies in a variety of capacities (Product Development, Operations, Business Development and Marketing) Michael was able to develop the ability to apply big picture thinking to very focused tasks. Capitalizing on this background Michael began helping private organizations (via www.ncompasscapital.ca) benefit from many of the strategic developments more commonly enjoyed by public companies with larger resource and talent pools.

Michael is a Professional Engineer, with an Honors Degree in Engineering Management from the Royal Military College of Canada, and a Certified Risk Manager.

Brian Hall,
Matrix POS

As this book goes to First Edition, I'm in the middle of a litigious situation – working through a bunch of things that I would have done differently – smarter – if I'd had Alizabeth's book a few years ago. Contract jurisdiction, for example – I would have known to pay attention to that clause in a supplier contract. Who'd have thought you could spend thousands of dollars in legal fees just trying to make it so that you can pursue a situation on your own turf?

The interesting thing about the battle that I'm in right now is that every small business person I talk to about it asks me the same question – "What did you learn?"

I learned three things. 1. Never – ever – leave the kids alone with someone who might talk them into doing stupid things. 2. Always make sure that you are seeing the information – business proof – that you should be seeing. No excuses. 3. Trust your gut.

201

In 2002, I was running and building a nice little business called Matrix, bringing cool IT solutions into the hospitality business in Canada. Lots of component parts involved – POS software, hardware, and support services. Most of the big solution vendors were in the US, and my local clients wanted solutions and commitments that were closer to them.

In 2001, a guy I knew was coming out of an ugly business situation – personal and corporate bankruptcy stuff – so I brought him in to work for me. Let's call him Guido. Over the next few years, Guido picked up the business well and gradually took on service and administration. Over time, I let Guido bring in another buddy of his – let's call him Bob – to help build the sales side and attract a new and a really major supplier.

In May 2005, I bought a second business – a floating hospitality venue that goes by the name of The Empress of Canada. I was really excited about that new adventure, and had all kinds of ideas I wanted to put into play, so that we could have a really successful first future.

Unbeknownst to me, my buddy Guido had been talking to my Empress partner, Mark (his real name). Guido had built Mark up to a froth on how much faster the Empress business would grow if I could spend all of my time working with him at the boat. So, when Guido suggested that he and Bob really could manage the Matrix business if I wanted to focus on the Empress – and Mark was really enthusiastic about me spending more time working with him – I went along with the suggestion.

About seven months later, I got a phone call from Guido telling me that he had sent me a letter and it was important that I read it. The letter was a blatant attempt to take over control of the business at far less than an even reasonable price. I was willing to consider selling, so I kept on taking the high road and made it clear I was receptive on the buy out but there was a big valuation gap. That was when Guido made it clear that he was leaving for a week's vacation, and unless he could buy me out for the price offered, he wouldn't be back. Good riddance, you say? Well, it got better.

Knowing that he was going to be away, I trundled on in to the office the next morning with the intent of settling things down while Guido and I sorted things out. That was when I realized that they had locked down all of the systems including the financial systems, and many of the recent prospective deals were, in fact, not signed on Matrix paper.

Fortunately I know lots of smart people, and we managed to get back in to all of the systems and take back control. We even found evidence of software shredding and other attempts to actually destroy Matrix assets. That was when we changed the locks – and got on with assessing the extent of the carnage.

It turns out that Guido and Bob had told the new large supplier we'd attracted and invested in heavily that they were buying us out. Guido and Bob convinced the new supplier that they should cancel Matrix as their local supplier and support them in setting up their own company to represent them. They had also held back millions of dollars in potential sales that they were not going to turn over to Matrix. The supplier really wanted an entry to the Canadian market, so they went along with Guido and Bob. Because we were not including their products in an upcoming trade show, they were planning to use that as a reason to cancel our dealership arrangement, also citing lack of sales as a significant issue. In fact, Guido and Bob had not made the trade show arrangements or closed any substantial deals in case they had to spin the company off on their own. We believe that the vendor's action against us was done in an effort to keep us from filing an injunction against them (which was exactly what we should have done). Big companies have big teams of lawyers – if you're going to deal with them, you need to know the contract and be prepared to act decisively. Don't take it personally.

Over the next few weeks, many of our long term employees left without notice – Bob included. With various vendors' help, we were able to put together most of the story, and we launched suit against Guido and Bob, the major supplier, and the new company they formed.

We're now into exactly the kind of contract nightmares Alizabeth talks about – one jurisdiction being in Texas, so potentially the whole thing has to be ruled on in Texas. Fortunately we had retained a specialized lawyer, and she found a new ruling that made it clear the case would get sent back to Canada where witnesses can be called.

History leaves clues. In retrospect, I had lots of things that should have given me cause to pause on the level of trust and control I had given Guido. For example, when he joined the company he put off signing any kind of non-compete and non-solicit – then the moment passed and it just never happened. Once I was working full time on the Empress, when I did come in I found more and more employees who were Guido's immediate family members. A couple of times when we were discussing legitimate sale opportunities of the business, he actually said "why would they buy something that they can just steal?"

If you want to be the kind of business person who operates on a reputation of integrity and respect, you have to work really hard to make sure that the rest of your team has the same core values – for the protection of your clients, your employees, and yourself.

Don't be naive. You've gotta think like a slime ball to work with a slime ball. Or you have to trust your instinct – I had this guy figured out a few years ago and should have gotten rid of him. In the absence of that, I needed Alizabeth's book a whole bunch sooner, so that I would have stuck to my instinct and not handed the business off before I had made sure that it was mature and sustainable.

Margaret Maich, How to Fire People

Every business goes through times when they must deal with the reality of letting people go… I deal with the people impacted by this - those who have lost their jobs – and how a business handles terminations is a key indicator of leadership maturity that every employee – the ones leaving AND the ones who remain, will take note of and remember. A mature business takes the time and makes the effort to be as respectful as possible of all their people, and a mature business leader pays attention to the things that will make this easier for the person being terminated.

I have been doing Career Transition work for 23 years and I must say that many, many organizations do a very good job of this very difficult task. They are thoughtful, careful and respectful. They think through and plan for every step of the process and as a result, they make the stark reality of being fired a little bit easier for the individual or individuals involved.

Of course, over that length of time I have seen and heard of some less-than-ideal situations: People fired by email, by a cell phone call while on vacation, or while driving home from work; or someone being fired the day before a landmark anniversary with the company, or on the anniversary of the death of their spouse; long-time employees required to clean out their desk on the spot and walk through the office carrying their boxes, or called in from a location 3 hours away and left with no way of getting back home when the company car was reclaimed. And we've had individuals who were given such a vague message that they didn't understand the import and asked me who I was and why I was there.

Reactions of individuals can span every conceivable emotion, from joy and relief to bitterness, anger or complete denial ("I need to get back to my desk, I have a meeting in half an hour!").

Following a few basic but essential tenets can truly help to make the best of a tough situation.

Respect for Privacy

Do everything you can to shield the employee from the public eye until they have had a chance to absorb the news, get over the initial shock and are at least in part, back to being the consummate professional they have always been.

As much as possible, deal with people as individuals – they've often worked for many years for the organization and are worthy of a little bit more of your time and attention as they receive this news.

If it's a group downsizing, do whatever is possible to ensure that individuals don't have to learn their fate in front of the entire employee population. ie. If you're in the unenviable position of having to hand out multiple packages at the same time, some that confirm continued employment and some that confirm termination, make sure that from the outside they look the same, thereby giving the individual a moment of privacy as they learn the news.

Respect for the People Involved

When you have to fire someone, to whatever extent possible, don't book the meeting ahead of time. Ascertain their whereabouts for "D" day to be sure that they'll be in the office and then call just shortly before the scheduled time and ask them to join you for a meeting. A few minutes or an hour of anxiety is far preferable to a night (or several days and nights!) of wondering and worrying.

Stick to the process set out by you and your HR team. If you happen to meet the individual earlier – at lunch or in the elevator – it might feel easier for you to 'get the news off your chest' then and there, but it's not easier for them. Follow the process so that the individual will have the time, information and support that they need and deserve. At the end of the day this is about them, it's not about anyone else.

Respect for the People Left Behind

Keep in mind that the people left behind will also be hurting. They have lost a close colleague or maybe a good friend. If this is a group downsizing, that just multiplies the impact. On top of that the 'survivors' often experience a degree of guilt that they still have a job while their colleague(s) does not, and a degree of worry as to whether they will be next.

Keep the lines of communication wide open. Be as transparent and upfront as you can be with the individual's team or the remaining employee population if that's appropriate. Tell them what's going on and the business reasons that necessitated it. Tell them what steps have been put in place to cover the work and publicly express your appreciation for the effort and contribution of those who have been let go.

If you want to have a sound base of people to grow with, you have to be respectful of all your people – even ones you are firing. If you do need to fire people, follow a few basic rules:

- *Plan it carefully and ahead of time, and stick to your plan.*

- *Train ALL staff involved.*

- *Do not pre-set the meeting or meetings in advance.*

- *Do it on a Tuesday, Wednesday or Thursday – early or late in the day.*

- *The immediate reporting manager should deliver the message whenever possible.*

- *Try to avoid working notice – let them leave immediately – this often feels cruel to an employer but it is kinder and more respectful in the long run.*

- *Use career transition support and if needed, lean on your provider to help coach the manager through this difficult conversation.*

- *Whenever possible, have the career transition consultant onsite at the time of the termination – this can make a world of difference to your employee. They will help them get through the initial shock and subsequent emotions and will ultimately, help the person to face forward toward the possibilities instead of back over their shoulder at what they've lost. We are the sliver of hope at a very bleak time in the individual's life.*

Margaret Maich's corporate experience in HR and HR executive management includes positions with Canada Life, Deloitte and Touche and finally, VP-HR at York Finch General Hospital. Her experience includes labour relations and contract negotiations, management and executive recruitment, corporate-wide retention strategies, implementing performance evaluation programs and planning and implementing organizational restructurings and downsizings. Margaret has over 20 years' consulting experience in career transition management, working one-on-one with executives. She has particular expertise in strategically positioning executives in the marketplace, fine tuning their networking and interview presentations and creating impactful written communications.

Margaret has served on the Board of Directors of the Human Resources Professionals Association of Ontario and has chaired their Annual Conference Committee. Margaret has an Honours Bachelor of Arts in English and History from Queen's University.

Grant Geminiuc,
How to Leverage Alternative
Staffing Models

Wikipedia defines outsourcing as subcontracting a process, such as product design or manufacturing, to a third-party company. They offer a long list of reasons why a company would outsource:

Cost savings *by addressing the scope and quality levels by enabling re-pricing, re-negotiation and cost re-structuring (including access to lower cost economies);* Focus on core business *(for example moving to specialized IT services companies);* Cost restructuring, *moving from fixed to variable cost and making variable costs more predictable;* Improved quality *by driving a specialized vendor to strong commitments through a service level agreement;* Knowledge, *including gaining access to intellectual property and wider experience;* Commitments, *moving to services governed by a legally binding performance contract with financial penalties and legal redress;* Operational best practice, *that would be too difficult or time consuming to develop in-house;* Access to a larger talent pool *and a sustainable source of skills;* Capacity management, *where the risk in providing the excess capacity is borne by the supplier;* Catalyst for change, *using the outsourcing agreement as a catalyst for major step change that can not be achieved alone;* Enhance capacity for innovation, *using external knowledge service providers to supplement limited in-house capacity for product innovation;* Reduced time to market, *effectively 'buying' ready to go development or production;* Standardization of business processes, *IT Services and application services, gaining access to services previously only available to large corporations;* Risk management, *partnering with an outsourcer who is better able to mitigate for known risks;* Capital investment, *leveraging private venture capital for startups in countries with private and government funds;* Tax benefits, *moving manufacturing operations to counter high corporate taxes.*

Outsourcing became part of the business lexicon during the 1980s. As much as it conjures passionate debates about job security and national pride, it is simply a division of labor that leverages some valuable business operations alternatives in an increasingly complicated technical world. Not to be entered into lightly, outsourcing in and of itself demands a focus on Growing Up.

We all agree that organizations travel through a maturity cycle based on their initial product set and target market. Entities that mature swiftly during market growth typically have the edge to lead the eventual market consolidation and take a dominant position. A small sub-set of these dominant industry players will use this rapid maturity capability to redefine the market landscape by expanding beyond the typical organic growth path. Based on size, leverage and brand recognition, these pioneers can rapidly move into new product categories, new customer formats, new geographic areas and new markets. However, to achieve sustained success in new frontiers often requires obtaining and maturing new capabilities to support execution.

Shoppers Drug Mart is a clear example of the type of maturity outlined above. Murray Koffler founded the company in 1962 and grew it through child and adolescent to a mature adult that eventually became the dominant player in the Canadian Drug Store chain industry. Each CEO since has been able to successfully lead the company into new frontiers while keeping true to the value proposition for clients and store associate pharmacists. So much has the company evolved that as of 2009, the company would be recognized in a larger industry category of health and beauty and would name Canadian Tire, Loblaws and WalMart among it's competitors.

Over the past four years, I have had the good fortune of advising, contributing and executing initiatives at Shoppers Drug Mart as Interim CIO and as an Executive Consultant.

With all the success and expansion, many new capabilities have been acquired along the journey. The challenge becomes one of HR portfolio management of corporate capabilities and their relative maturity visa via the competitive marketplace to sustain market dominance. It is an on-going challenge for successful and evolving companies, like Shoppers Drug Mart to identify which corporate capabilities are market differentiators (versus commodity) based on their value proposition. Current CEO, Jürgen Schreiber brings a clear vision to which corporate capabilities are strategic and has made investments in an executive team that can accelerate their maturation.

In 2003, Shoppers began to look differently at IT operations – recognizing that IT is critically important to the business operations of stores. IT was also recognized as a commodity capability that could be scaled and provided more cost-effectively by one or more third party service providers. What was not well understood at that time was that in the process of buying that capability from a third party vendor, they would have to develop a new capability – how to manage a complex services vendor. *A new capability was required – vendor governance.*

As with most new capabilities, it does not matter how successful and sophisticated an entity is, a new capability requires starting from first principles and going through the maturity curve with all stakeholders: IT, legal, HR, procurement & real estate.

The rest of this article talks to the maturing of the vendor governance capability at Shoppers. Each outsourcing arrangement is like a child being born that has to go through the maturity stages during the life of the deal. Within outsourcing it is not uncommon that adolescence is the best that can be obtained during the 1st term (3-5 years) of the deal. Subsequent re-scoped extensions or new deals may be required to achieve full expectations of adulthood. With that said, most organizations are likely to launch another outsourcing deal, like another child after they are comfortable with the first child after 1 or 2 years. Your outsourcing capability is in full swing when you have a family mix of baby, adolescent and adult outsourcing arrangements. The challenge and opportunity is to understand the uniqueness and differences and manage them accordingly.

In the case of Shoppers, they initiated the first outsourcing initiative for IT – focusing on managed applications (software) with AMS Outsourcer in July, 2004. As with a 1st child, there were a lot of surprises, learnings and frustrations from the new parent that did not know what to expect – not that different than most first-time outsourcing deals.

In this arrangement, the first year was very difficult. The challenges seem to arise mainly from a difficult child and a parental response of doing everything for the child. The outsourcer was not well structured, motivated or directed. Shoppers chose to respond by more actively managing and doing the outsourcer's tasks rather then establish and enforce governance to achieve the outcomes expected. This strong parental response lead to friction and sub-optimal performance. With this rocky start, the outsourcing arrangement did mature eventually into full adulthood, but it took more patience and persistence than might have been the case if proper governance had been in place from the start.

Outsourcing is not a 'deal,' it's a relationship. As such, you can think of the growth path in terms of exactly the growth events that Alizabeth decribes:

- Toddler (The first 1-2 years of an outsourcing relationship)

    o Services Being Delivered - Closely monitored activity and performance with tight controls until client feels comfortable the vendor can perform the various services – like security gates.

    o SLAs Established - Initially receive baseline data and SLA reports that are not well understood, reliable or validated – your trust level starts low. Take the time to go through with the vendor the definition of all activities, how data is captured and reported so everyone is one the same page. Establish a validation model that is baked into the standard process for these reports. Once established you can put in place appropriate controls to ensure validation is working and reports are accurate.

    o Stakeholders engaged – Often overlooked, but very important for success is stakeholder engagement and organizational change management during this stage. A new target operating model must be established and a reasonable timetable to transition from current state. Appropriate support must also be provided during the difficult change so feelings of loss of control can be addressed and resolved.

- Adolescent stage (3-4 years into the relationship)
  o Service Improvement - Matching supply to the customer demand via mature planning/ scheduling and skills coverage based on cross training; Identifying root cause issues to re-occurring incidents and providing basic analytics capabilities
  o SLA Met - Rarely are SLA reports or statements misunderstood; At this stage, the outsourcer is providing a remedy for any missed SLAs in an timely and acceptable fashion.
  o Customer Feedback loop – Customer satisfaction surveys and meetings are providing tangible feedback that are being addressed with appropriate actions plans.

- Adult stage (5 yr and into extension 6-7 years of an outsourcing relationship)
  o Continuous Improvement – Some combination of Quality of service, SLAs and price are in a continuous improvement cycle now that the levers are well understood and working to achieve improvements. Typically advanced analytics are in place.

o   No Surprises – Operations are as expected
with little surprises

Like the 2nd child , the second outsourcing
arrangement is easier. Shoppers leveraged what they learned
in their applications relationship as the basis for planning and
negotiating a managed network service arrangement last year.
The initiative moved quickly to a stable relationship, meeting
the definition of adolescence – and the more mature business
expectations – in a much shorter timeframe.

*Now Shoppers are on to having their 3rd child. This one
will be the poor kid who's never photographed because mom and
dad are too busy just getting on with it. The oldest children will
often tell you that they had to forge the way – they fought all the
battles – and the younger children reap the benefit in an easier and
much less painful path to independence. So too in outsourcing,
as Shoppers begins pursuing a hardware maintenance outsourcing
relationship. In this third outsourcing program, Shoppers can
begin to leverage the lessons they've learned and be the more
calm and relaxed parents by creating a common and sustainable
governance framework for all of their outsourced relationships.*

 Mr. Geminiuc is Managing Director of R3P Consulting founded in 2008. A strategist and program executive that specializes in large consolidation, merger & acquisition, outsourcing initiatives and IT vendor management. He has advised on some of the largest outsourcing deals in Canada, established several IT vendor management offices, acted as Interim CIO for Shoppers Drug Mart and has overseen 100+ consolidations and transitions. He can be reached at ggeminiuc@r3pconsultants. com or through his website www.r3pconsultants.com. Mr. Geminiuc holds a BMATH from University of Waterloo and enjoys golfing, skiing, aviation and spending time with his two young children and wife.

About the Author

Alizabeth Calder has been recognized as an entertaining and insightful speaker for close to 30 years. A former Fortune 500 executive, she now applies her energy, and her wit, to the challenge of extracting the practical kernels of management practice that are needed in even the smallest of companies. A values-based, strategic leader, Alizabeth's consulting clients look to her for the ability to set vision and direction, build a cohesive team and motivate to achieve superior results. She works with CEO's, Boards of Directors, and Venture Capitalists, assessing the operational and business elements of key investments, defining effective governance programs to reduce risk and ensure success.

To learn more, please visit Alizabeth's website at: **www.alizabethcalder.com.**

Notes

Introduction
[1] Mark McNeilly, *Sun Tzu and the Art of Business* (Oxford, 1996)

Chapter One
[2] Steven S. Little, *The Milkshake Moment; Overcoming Stupid Systems, Pointless Policies, and Muddled Management to Realize Real Growth* (Wiley & Sons Inc, 2008), p 31.

[3] Lou V. Gerstner Jr., *Who Says Elephants Can't Dance?* (Harper Collins Publishers, 2002), p 73.

Chapter Two
[4] Sal Severe, PhD, *How to Behave So Your Children Will Too* (Penguin Books, 1997), p 57.

[5] Hara Estroff Marano, *A Nation of Wimps; The High Cost of Invasive Parenting* (Broadway Books, 2008), p 258 – 259.

Chapter Three

[6] Ronald G. Morrish, *The Secrets of Discipline* (Woodstream Publishing, 1987), p 62.

[7] Ronald G. Morrish, *The Secrets of Discipline* (Woodstream Publishing, 1987), p 13.

[8] Ronald G. Morrish, *The Secrets of Discipline* (Woodstream Publishing, 1987), p 64.

Chapter Four

[9] Ronald G. Morrish, *The Secrets of Discipline* (Woodstream Publishing, 1987), p 71.

Chapter Five

[10] Ronald G. Morrish, *The Secrets of Discipline* (Woodstream Publishing, 1987), p 28.

[11] Steven R. Rayner, *Recreating the Workplace; the Pathway to High Performance Work Systems* (Oliver Wright Publications, 1993), p 132—133.

[12] Hara Estroff Marano, *A Nation of Wimps; The High Cost of Invasive Parenting* (Broadway Books, 2008), p 262.

Chapter Six

[13] Stephan H. Haeckel, *The Adaptive Enterprise; Creating and Leading Sense and Respond Organizations* (Harvard Business School Press, 1999), p 77.

[14] Lou V. Gerstner Jr., *Who Says Elephants Can't Dance?* (Harper Collins Publishers, 2002), p 67.

[15] Chris Zook with James Allen, *Profit From The Core* (Harvard Business School Press, 2001).

[16] Hara Estroff Marano, *A Nation of Wimps; The High Cost of Invasive Parenting* (Broadway Books, 2008), p 261.

Chapter Seven

[17] Ronald G. Morrish, *The Secrets of Discipline* (Woodstream Publishing, 1987), p 69.

[18] Richard S. Wellins, William C. Byham, Jeanne M. Wilson, *Empowered Teams; Creating Self-Directed Work Groups That Improve Quality, Productivity and Participation* (Jossey-Bass Inc, 1991) p. 188.

[19] Richard S. Wellins, William C. Byham, Jeanne M. Wilson, *Empowered Teams; Creating Self-Directed Work Groups That Improve Quality, Productivity and Participation* (Jossey-Bass Inc, 1991) p. 189.

[20] Hara Estroff Marano, *A Nation of Wimps; The High Cost of Invasive Parenting* (Broadway Books, 2008), p 257.

Chapter Eight

[21] Steven R. Rayner, *Recreating the Workplace; the Pathway to High Performance Work Systems* (Oliver Wright Publications, 1993), p 69.

Chapter Nine

[22] Douglas K. Smith, *Taking Charge of Change; 10 Principles for Managing People and Performance* (Addison-Wesley Publishing Company, 1996), p 285.

[23] Hara Estroff Marano, *A Nation of Wimps; The High Cost of Invasive Parenting* (Broadway Books, 2008), p 261.

Chapter Ten

[24] Sal Severe, PhD, *How to Behave So Your Children Will Too* (Penguin Books, 1997), p 259.

[25] Steven S. Little, *The Milkshake Moment; Overcoming Stupid Systems, Pointless Policies, and Muddled Management to Realize Real Growth* (Wiley & Sons Inc, 2008) p. 31—36.

[26] Bettie B. Youngs, Joanne Wolf, Joani Wafer, Dawn Lehman, *Teaching Kids to Care* (Hampton Roads Publishing, 2007) p.25—27.

Chapter Eleven

[27] Bryce Webster, *Winner Take All* (American Management Association, 1987), p37.

[28] Martin R. Smith, *I Hate to See a Manager Cry; How to Prevent the Litany of Management From Fouling Up Your Career* (Addison-Wesley Publishing Co, 1964) p.29.

[29] Hara Estroff Marano, *A Nation of Wimps; The High Cost of Invasive Parenting* (Broadway Books, 2008), p259.

[30] Philip B. Crosby, *Quality is Free* (Mentor Publishing, 1980) p.13.

[31] Steven S. Little, *The Milkshake Moment; Overcoming Stupid Systems, Pointless Policies, and Muddled Management to Realize Real Growth* (Wiley & Sons Inc, 2008) p.89.

[32] Bryce Webster, *Winner Take All* (American Management Association, 1987) p.27.

[33] Tom Peters, *Thriving on Chaos* (Harper & Row, 1987) p.379.

[34] Tom Peters, *Thriving on Chaos* (Harper & Row, 1987) p.539.

[35] Steven R. Covey, *The 7 Habits of Highly Effective People* (Simon & Schuster, 1989) p.193.

[36] Steven R. Rayner, *Recreating the Workplace; the Pathway to High Performance Work Systems* (Oliver Wright Publications, 1993), p.106.

[37] Stephan H. Haeckel, *The Adaptive Enterprise; Creating and Leading Sense and Respond Organizations* (Harvard Business School Press, 1999), p.150.

[38] Stephan H. Haeckel, *The Adaptive Enterprise; Creating and Leading Sense and Respond Organizations* (Harvard Business School Press, 1999), p.225—226.

[39] Roger Fisher, William Ury, Bruce Patton, *Getting to Yes* (Penguin Books, 1991), p.4.

[40] Sal Severe, PhD, *How to Behave So Your Children Will Too* (Penguin Books, 1997), p.259.

[41] Harvey MacKay, *Beware the Naked Man Who Offers You His Shirt; Do What You Love, Love What You Do and Deliver What You Promise* (William Morrow and Company, 1990), p.133.

[42] David Novak, *The Education of an Accidental CEO; Lessons Learned From the Trailer Park to the Corner Office* (Crown Publishing 2007), p.46.

[43] Daniel Goleman, *Working With Emotional Intelligence* (Bantam Books, 1998), p.51.

[44] Daniel Goleman, *Working With Emotional Intelligence* (Bantam Books, 1998), p.61.

[45] Hara Estroff Marano, *A Nation of Wimps; The High Cost of Invasive Parenting* (Broadway Books, 2008), p.256.

Chapter Twelve

[46] Sal Severe, PhD, *How to Behave So Your Children Will Too* (Penguin Books, 1997), p.16.

[47] Ronald G. Morrish, *The Secrets of Discipline* (Woodstream Publishing, 1987), p.96.

[48] Steven S. Little, *The Milkshake Moment; Overcoming Stupid Systems, Pointless Policies, and Muddled Management to Realize Real Growth* (Wiley & Sons Inc, 2008) p.71.

[49] Tom Peters, *Thriving on Chaos* (Harper & Row, 1987) p.585.

[50] Harvey MacKay, *Beware the Naked Man Who Offers You His Shirt* (William Morrow and Company, 1990), p.128.

[51] Sal Severe, PhD, *How to Behave So Your Children Will Too* (Penguin Books, 1997), p.4.

[52] Hara Estroff Marano, *A Nation of Wimps; The High Cost of Invasive Parenting* (Broadway Books, 2008), p.261-262.

[53] Stephan H. Haeckel, *The Adaptive Enterprise; Creating and Leading Sense and Respond Organizations* (Harvard Business School Press, 1999), p.xii.

[54] Steven S. Little, *The Milkshake Moment; Overcoming Stupid Systems, Pointless Policies, and Muddled Management to Realize Real Growth* (Wiley & Sons Inc, 2008) p.149.

[55] Sal Severe, PhD, *How to Behave So Your Children Will Too* (Penguin Books, 1997), p.40.

[56] Steven S. Little, *The Milkshake Moment; Overcoming Stupid Systems, Pointless Policies, and Muddled Management to Realize Real Growth* (Wiley & Sons Inc, 2008) p.129.

[57] Steven R. Covey, *The 7 Habits of Highly Effective People* (Simon & Schuster, 1989) p.193.

[58] Steven R. Covey, *The 7 Habits of Highly Effective People* (Simon & Schuster, 1989) p.190—197.

[59] David Novak, *The Education of an Accidental CEO; Lessons*

Learned From the Trailer Park to the Corner Office
(Crown Publishing 2007), p.80.

[60] Steven S. Little, *The Milkshake Moment; Overcoming Stupid
Systems, Pointless Policies, and Muddled Management to
Realize Real Growth* (Wiley & Sons Inc, 2008) p.47.

[61] Sal Severe, PhD, *How to Behave So Your Children Will Too*
(Penguin Books, 1997), p.10.

[62] Daniel Goleman, *Working With Emotional Intelligence*
(Bantam Books, 1998), p.54.

[63] Karl F. Gretz and Steven R. Drozdeck, *Empowering
Innovative People; How Managers Challenge, Channel
and Control the Truly Creative and Talented* (Probus
Publishing Company 1992), p.107—111.

Chapter Thirteen

[64] Tom Peters, *Thriving on Chaos* (Harper & Row, 1987) p.45.

[65] Tom Peters, *Thriving on Chaos* (Harper & Row, 1987) p.53.

[66] Karl F. Gretz and Steven R. Drozdeck, *Empowering
Innovative People; How Managers Challenge, Channel
and Control the Truly Creative and Talented* (Probus
Publishing Company 1992), p.17.

[67] Ronald G. Morrish, *The Secrets of Discipline* (Woodstream
Publishing, 1987), p.29.

[68] Stephan H. Haeckel, *The Adaptive Enterprise; Creating and
Leading Sense and Respond Organizations* (Harvard
Business School Press, 1999), p.xii.

[69] Lou V. Gerstner Jr., *Who Says Elephants Can't Dance?* (Harper
Collins Publishers, 2002), p.123.

[70] Michael L. Tushman and Charles A. O'Reilly III, *Winning Through Innovation; A Practical Guide to Leading Organizational Change and Renewal* (Harvard Business School Press, 1997, 2002), p.131.

[71] Stephan H. Haeckel, *The Adaptive Enterprise; Creating and Leading Sense and Respond Organizations* (Harvard Business School Press, 1999), p.95.

[72] Steven S. Little, *The Milkshake Moment; Overcoming Stupid Systems, Pointless Policies, and Muddled Management to Realize Real Growth* (Wiley & Sons Inc, 2008) p.83.

[73] Michael Maquardt, *Leading With Questions; How Leaders Find the Right Solutions By Knowing What to Ask* (Jossey-Bass, 2005), p.19.

[74] Stephan H. Haeckel, *The Adaptive Enterprise; Creating and Leading Sense and Respond Organizations* (Harvard Business School Press, 1999), p.103.

Chapter Fourteen

[75] Michael L. Tushman and Charles A. O'Reilly III, *Winning Through Innovation; A Practical Guide to Leading Organizational Change and Renewal* (Harvard Business School Press, 1997, 2002), p.36.

[76] Lou V. Gerstner Jr., *Who Says Elephants Can't Dance?* (Harper Collins Publishers, 2002), p.205.

[77] Lou V. Gerstner Jr., *Who Says Elephants Can't Dance?* (Harper Collins Publishers, 2002), p.316.

[78] Lou V. Gerstner Jr., *Who Says Elephants Can't Dance?* (Harper Collins Publishers, 2002), p.210.

[79] Roger Fisher, Willian Ury and Bruce Patton, *Getting to Yes* (Penguin Books, 1991), p.109.

[80] Mark H. McCormack, *What They Still Don't Teach You at Harvard Business School* (Bantam Books), p.91—92.

Appendix

[81] Roger Martin, *The Opposable Mind; Winning Through Integrative Thinking* (Harvard Publishing, 2009)

[82] Keith Damsell, "Succesion Issues Cause for Concern; CanWest head's death sends media giant into uncertainty" in *The Globe and Mail* (Oct. 8, 2003).

Did you like this book?

If you enjoyed this book, you will find more
interesting books at

www.MMPubs.com

Please take the time to let us know how
you liked this book. Even short reviews of 2-3
sentences can be helpful and may be used in our
marketing materials. If you take the time to post a
review for this book on Amazon.com, let us know
when the review is posted and you will receive a
free audiobook or ebook from our catalog. Simply
email the link to the review once it is live on
Amazon.com, with your name, and your mailing
address—send the email to orders@mmpubs.
com with the subject line "Book Review Posted on
Amazon."

If you have questions about this book, our
customer loyalty program, or our review rewards
program, please contact us at info@mmpubs.com.

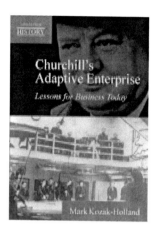

Churchill's Adaptive Enterprise: Lessons for Business Today

This book analyzes a period of time from World War II when Winston Churchill, one of history's most famous leaders, faced near defeat for the British in the face of sustained German attacks. The book describes the strategies he used to overcome incredible odds and turn the tide on the impending invasion. The historical analysis is done through a modern business and information technology lens, describing Churchill's actions and strategy using modern business tools and techniques. Aimed at business executives, IT managers, and project managers, the book extracts learnings from Churchill's experiences that can be applied to business problems today. Particular themes in the book are knowledge management, information portals, adaptive enterprises, and organizational agility.

Eric Hoffer Book Award (2007) Winner

ISBN: 1-895186-19-6   (paperback)

Also available in ebook formats. Order from your local bookseller, Amazon.com, or directly from the publisher at **http://www.mmpubs.com/churchill**

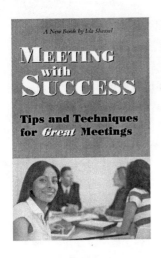

By Peter R. Garber

Want to Get Ahead in Your Career?

Do you find yourself challenged by office politics, bad things happen-ing to good careers, dealing with the "big cheeses" at work, the need for effective networking skills, and keeping good working relation-ships with coworkers and bosses? *Winning the Rat Race at Work* is a unique book that provides you with case studies, interactive exercises, self-assessments, strategies, evaluations, and models for overcoming these workplace challenges. The book illustrates the stages of a career and the career choices that determine your future, empowering you to make positive changes.

Written by Peter R. Garber, the author of *100 Ways to Get on the Wrong Side of Your Boss*, this book is a must read for anyone interested in getting ahead in his or her career. You will want to keep a copy in your top desk drawer for ready reference whenever you find yourself in a challenging predicament at work.

ISBN: 1-895186-68-4   (paperback)

Also available in ebook formats. Order from your local bookseller, Amazon.com, or directly from the publisher at **http://www.mmpubs.com/rats**

Need More Help with the Politics at Work?

100 Ways To Get On The Wrong Side Of Your Boss (And Strategies to Prevent You from Getting There!) was written for anyone who has ever been frustrated by his or her working relationship with the boss—and who hasn't ever felt this way! Bosses play a critically important role in your career success and getting on the wrong side of this important individual in your working life is not a good thing.

Each of these 100 Ways is designed to illustrate a particular problem that you may encounter when dealing with your boss and then an effective strategy to prevent this problem from reoccurring. You will learn how to deal more effectively with your boss in this fun and practical book filled with invaluable advice that can be utilized every day at work.

Written by Peter R. Garber, the author of *Winning the Rat Race at Work*, this book is a must read for anyone inter-ested in getting ahead. You will want to keep a copy in your top desk drawer for ready reference whenever you find yourself in a challenging predicament at work.

ISBN: 1-895186-98-6   (paperback)

Also available in ebook formats. Order from your local bookseller, Amazon.com, or directly from the publisher at **http://www.InTroubleAtWork.com**

LaVergne, TN USA
14 October 2009
160772LV00001B/2/P